Reoffending:

A practitioner's guide to working with offenders and offending behaviour in the Criminal Justice System

by Jonathan Hussey

BENNION KEARNY

To my family.

No words can come close to how appreciative I am of your continuous support, love and encouragement. You truly are my rock. I dedicate the completion of this book to you.

Acknowledgements

In addition to my family, there are a few individuals in particular whom I would like to thank personally for their help during my journey of completing this book.

Olivia Collingwood - thank you for your support and belief in me. You are an incredible individual who has always kept me focused on my goals. You are an inspiration to those working in this field with your ideas.

Mark Cawdell, Sarah Cunnington, and Saiqa Yasmin - my great, loyal friends - you are very special people and have helped me greatly. And Mark, I guess in times of difficulty, there really is opportunity like you said. I guess you just have to look in the right direction and persevere.

Jo Richardson - your contribution to this book can only be described as outstanding. Thank you so much!

Martyn Waters - for all the times you have helped me over the years especially with this project, thank you!

My Publisher - special thanks for all your hard work and support from the start.

And lastly, but importantly, to my clients. This book would be impossible without the experiences you have given me.

About the Author

Jonathan Hussey is one of the most exciting innovators of interventions for rehabilitating offenders today. He holds a B.Sc. (Hons) in Psychology from Loughborough University and a B.A. (Hons) in Community Justice Studies from Portsmouth University, as well as being a fully qualified, experienced, and award winning Probation Officer.

Jonathan has worked extensively in the Criminal Justice System, but has specialized in leading roles within the Probation Service and Youth Offending Services. In doing so, Jonathan has assisted and helped change the lives of many offenders, influenced organizational change, and mentored colleagues.

Jonathan currently works as a consultant for the Probation Service, and has established a successful training company; Intervention Consultancy (www.intervention-consultancy.co.uk). Here he provides bespoke training packages, life coaching, mentoring, seminars and specialist interventions across the country.

Jonathan spends time as a speaker at universities, colleges, schools and various criminal justice system organizations. His passion is simple: he intends to share the knowledge that really helps people change their lives for the better.

About the Reviewers

Mark Cawdell is currently working as a Probation Officer, and Learning and Development Officer for Thames Valley Probation Trust. In this role he mentors and assesses both Probation Service Officers and those training to become Probation Officers. Mark has been an experienced officer for many years having significant experience in working with high risk cases including sex offenders and those with substance misuse problems within a multi-agency setting. Mark holds a BSc (Hons) Social Policy, Loughborough; MSc Criminology and Criminal Justice, Loughborough; and a BA (Hons) Community Justice, Portsmouth and is a well-respected practitioner in the service today.

Jo Richardson joined the Probation Service in 2005, initially within the Employment, Training and Education team before working as a Probation Officer from 2006. She is currently employed by the Thames Valley Probation Trust and works within the generic team managing offenders who pose medium or high risk of serious harm to the public. She is trained as an Aggression Replacement Training (ART) facilitator, delivering this to both male and female offenders. Both her roles within the Probation Service have involved a high level of multi-agency working, including increasing the awareness of other agencies to the role of the Probation Service.

Martyn Waters is a qualified youth worker with 20 years of experience in the Third Sector including five years as a volunteer with Buckinghamshire Youth Offending Service. He joined the Probation Service in 2006 and now works as a Probation Officer with Thames Valley Probation Trust. He has a wide experience of offender management both in the community and within the prison estate. Previously he has managed a mixed caseload of offenders including those who pose a high risk of serious harm to members of the public, and worked with generic cases and within a multi-agency setting (Integrated Offender Management). Martyn is currently on secondment as a Probation Officer at a Young Offenders Institution (YOI).

Table of Contents

Preface   1

Introduction   5

Chapter 1 - Entering the Criminal Justice System   7

Chapter 2 - The Working Relationship   23

Chapter 3 - Working with Individuals who Offend and Misuse Substances   53

Chapter 4 - Working with Domestic Abuse   79

Chapter 5 - Working with Violent Offenders   105

Chapter 6 - Working with Sex Offenders   127

Chapter 7 - Working with Offenders with Emotional Problems   149

Chapter 8 - Tips   171

Bibliography   191

Preface

Working with offending behaviour is one of the most complex psychological roles for professionals today. Empowering people to change their behaviour is even more complicated. So my work aim is simple: to try and make the journey for the offender and practitioner a little easier along each unique path of change.

Reflecting upon the events that led me to begin the journey of writing this book, I can only describe the preceding events of my own path as life changing. Therefore, as a means of giving back to those who have helped me, I hope to inspire and contribute to the ever progressing and changing work being undertaken with offenders today. Additionally, I want to reflect and adapt some of the skills, techniques and knowledge others have taught me as a form of thanks and gratitude.

Expressing my appreciation through my writing is especially pertinent given that the professionals, who have helped me, as well as others in these occupations, often receive little or no praise for the hard work they do.

In many ways I feel that this book, metaphorically speaking anyway, is an extension of how I perceive we should address offending behaviour from what I have learnt on the front line. Over the coming pages I will disclose and discuss my own personal experiences of what I have found to be effective (and not so effective) in my practice. I do this by analysing true life (anonymised) case studies, exercises, and strategies that have worked for me with some of the most difficult clients imaginable.

It is at this point that I would like to make it crystal clear that this book is written as my own professional reflections only, and has not been commissioned by any professional government bodies. Nor does it intentionally reflect the views or agenda of any particular establishment. I hope that this book can be used as an aid to help practitioners already working within professional organisations, and I would like this book to act as a trigger of some sort to inspire those looking to work with offenders.

Who This Book is For

Reoffending is aimed at readers beginning their careers of working with offenders in the Probation Service and Youth Offending Service. The book is based predominately on my own experiences as a professional who works with offending behaviour. My experiences stem from having worked both in lead roles in the Probation Service and the Youth Offending Services, and I have been extensively involved in the implementation and design of various programmes to address offending behaviour. I have also worked as both a mentor and assessor for these organisations.

My main experience, however, has been working on a one-to-one basis with 'low to high' risk offenders in the community and within the prison system. I have been privileged to work alongside some brilliant professionals delivering programmes which have both inspired me and assisted me through some difficult times, difficult times which - I believe - all practitioners will most likely face at one time or another. This extends to individuals not only in the Probation and Youth Offending Service but also individuals in the police, social care, and the voluntary sector.

Having worked so extensively with such first rate professionals, and having been lucky to experience such a breadth of roles and challenges, this book is deeply personal to me and so in many ways I hope to reflect the struggles of on-going dedicated professionals who continue in these roles. My wish is that in some way, I can assist them, as well as newcomers to the profession. I do not feel that roles which deal with offending behaviour should be taken lightly; they are in fact *life-changing!* The emotional and practical impact of working in this challenging arena should be fully recognised before anyone seeks to turn their hand to it. In fact, later in the book, I will dedicate a whole chapter to safeguarding the practitioner and tips for survival.

What This Book Covers

I have broken the book down into 8 chapters. Each chapter will look at a different subject.

Although the book can be read non-sequentially, I recommend that you read chapters one and two first. Following this, feel free to dip in and out of chapters depending on your need. Why do I feel it important to read chapters one and two? Because these two chapters will provide you with what I feel is the essential foundation knowledge for starting to work with any offender.

Chapter 1 describes how individuals who commit crime may become involved with professionals who address offending behaviour. It then looks at the assessments made by such professionals and the problems and implications these have. Following this, I look at how to start to address offending behaviour and the forms and types of interventions that are put in place. Here I will also reflect on some of the issues raised. Incorporated within the subsections of each chapter are a number of tips to help the practitioner including: making accurate assessments, intervention planning, and goal setting.

Chapter 2 details the importance of the working relationship between the offender and the working professional. I will overview *why* this is important, and propose methods of working with offenders to assist building trusting relationships, as well as looking at what is already being used. Again, I will provide the reader with advice to guide them and assist them through some of the issues that they may face. Critically, I also introduce the reader to the essential knowledge of the "cycle of change" and motivational interviewing while giving clear guidance on how to execute these skills. Also look out for my tips on how to supercharge the working relationship.

Chapter 3 provides an overview of how practitioners in the Criminal Justice System work with offenders who misuse both alcohol and drugs; specifically focusing on how this is achieved by the Probation Service and Youth Offending Service. This chapter is divided into two main sections. Part one focuses on alcohol, part two on drugs. Within these sections, I look at providing context to these problems and how to address them. This chapter looks in detail at addictive behaviour and the implications this can have on offending behaviour. I will suggest ways of working with such individuals within the scope of what is possible within time bound constraints.

Chapter 4 looks at how to address domestic abuse with adult male offenders. Here I will talk about the skills needed to work with this typology and then discuss the offender's journey within the Criminal Justice System. I shall also address assessing risk and interventions with these offenders, as well as highlighting the signs that practitioners should pick up on - as they are linked to further abuse.

Chapter 5 addresses the subject of working with violent offenders and how best to minimise the risks they may pose. In order to do this, I discuss and describe exercises I have used with my clients to help change their thinking processes. The chapter then moves on to highlight some of the most pertinent factors I have seen linked to violent crime.

Chapter 6 explores my experiences of working with adult male sex offenders. Here I reflect on case studies and exercises I have used with my cases and critically assess their effectiveness and how I have used theory in my assessment of these cases.

Chapter 7 addresses two of the most common emotional wellbeing issues I am faced with on a day-to-day basis: depression and anxiety. In this chapter, I will focus on how to recognise the signs of depression and anxiety as well as how to put in place effective methods to help offenders cope with these sometimes crippling problems. These exercises are also transferable to the practitioner should they feel low or down.

Chapter 8 looks conclusively at specific guidance for protecting the practitioner. I will look at methods you can employ to safeguard yourself. I feel that if you are practising at the moment, then this chapter will be of great significance to you - as I share some of the best advice I can offer on working within the Criminal Justice System.

A Couple of Points

It is worth making clear that I have had to be careful with some potential issues of language. Firstly, I interchangeably use the terms: *offender*, *patient* and *client* and the chosen term depends on the context in which I am writing. For all the various possible interpretations and connotations, these terms are simply used in relation to the *individual receiving the intervention.* They are descriptive terms which I use to explain my points. Moreover, they are only some of the terms that are currently used within the Criminal Justice System.

The second problem is with the terms "she" or "he" - used to refer to the gender of an individual. I may interchange these terms during the text. However this is to help assist with the confidentiality of the case examples I am discussing. At some points, I will discuss working with specific genders and these examples will be clearly identified.

Feedback

In many ways, this book represents a personal perspective. Other practitioners may hold different positions and viewpoints. I am very interested in hearing from people who would like to comment on this book and I would like to invite you to leave feedback on:

www.reoffending.org.uk

This site will, hopefully, become a valuable resource in addition to the book.

Introduction

The critical question of this book and of ever increasing importance in society today is *how do we address offending behaviour*? Then we may ask, if we can understand the reasons *why* people commit crime and act in an antisocial manner, *why* are such things so difficult to stop?

Various approaches have been used over time but at the point of writing this book Cognitive Behavioural Treatment (CBT) has been shown to be the most effective (evidence based) form. Current practices within the Criminal Justice System (CJS) tend to utilise CBT in one form or another, and so CBT fundamentally underpins the service that individuals receive.

In this book, I do not intend to comprehensively address whether CBT really is the most effective method of addressing offending behaviour from the many other theoretical standpoints and approaches. My intention is simply to inform the reader of what issues they may face in specific areas, what skills have worked for me, and then provide tips on working with the different types of offenders to ensure that you (as you embark on a career in this field) deliver the best possible service.

Within this book, I intend to share various case studies as examples to show how different interventions have, or have not, worked for me. I believe that by sharing this information, the reader will be able to prepare themselves for the problems they might encounter. After all, forewarned is forearmed!

A word or two of warning: this book does not give a comprehensive account or step-by-step methodology in how to address offending behaviour. Its aim is more to provide some useful ideas and strategies to prompt and inspire the practitioner or budding professionals.

When considering the different theoretical frameworks, I am convinced that the many different approaches are helpful and will work for different people. However my focus will be on CBT. In my experience, I believe that CBT does make a valuable contribution to addressing offending behaviour, and in bringing about change. But, from what I have seen, the client needs to be motivated for it to actually work. The client may also need a positive support network of family or friends who can support them through the learning process. This is because many of the skills being taught are written exercises, role play, and homework.

Taking this reflection one step further - when considering the effectiveness of CBT - I often think about other considerations. For example, how can practitioners apply CBT to offenders who have limited or no motivation, no positive networks, and who are not willing to change because they controversially 'enjoy the lifestyle their offending brings'? Hopefully, I can give the reader some insights on how to work with this resistance.

Addressing offending behaviour has to be one of the most complex and difficult subjects to tackle. It is a pandemic problem in society and every country has its own perspectives and approaches. Addressing offending behaviour is therefore affected by individual approaches, local policies, government initiatives, legislation and law.

This book will look at offending behaviour and how it is addressed from my experiences within a British culture. It does however draw upon some useful research from America. I feel that it is important to highlight this as some of the methodologies and research used may not be applicable to other countries outside these regions. However, given that Britain is a multicultural society - this book should, in my view, have some standing within other countries.

As stated previously, this book is hugely important to me. I want to be able to help individuals move away from crime and lead better lives. I also want to share and voice the practitioner's struggles and successes. What I do not want is for the reader to feel as though I know all the answers. I do not. What I do have, however, is experience and an understanding of what works currently in my practice on the front line.

If you are an individual reading this book, using this as a form of 'instruction manual' to offending behaviour, then please stop now. This is not for you. This book can however be used as a guide and prompt for those currently working with offending behaviour. Hopefully, it will also act as a motivational tool to inspire those considering professions in this field.

It is my overall belief that practitioners currently addressing offending behaviour can, and are, reducing offending behaviour. They are also, in many cases, doing a truly excellent job. This is a difficult task, and by reading this book I hope to make the process a little easier and maybe even fun!

1

Entering the Criminal Justice System

Change for anyone can be difficult. But change for offenders, as they look to move away from offending behaviour, can be even harder as many individuals may not want to change, or do not feel that they can. There are, however, specially trained individuals in different organisations such as the Probation Service and Youth Offending Service (YOS) who try to empower people and help make change happen. Here, I will begin to explain how they seek to do this.

I will start by leading the reader along one of (what I call) the 'rehabilitative paths' that an offender may be encouraged to take after being charged with an offence. I will also explain some of the ways that courts make the decision to impose a path if they receive a report from the Probation Service or YOS. Following this, I will begin to explain how practitioners ensure that they make sound and justified assessments, and offer some useful advice and tips.

As part of the assessment process, the Probation Service or YOS will propose a plan that details what is considered to be the best way to change an individual's offending behaviour. The plan also assists the court in deciding on the appropriateness of rehabilitative disposals. Looking at these plans, I will offer some advice and experiences on how to make them more effective and also look to explore how we can work with unmotivated offenders. In parts, this chapter may feel as though it focuses on the 'negative' during discussions of assessments – but this is not my intention. My intention is simply to promote positive change through reflection.

The professionals who address offending behaviour, and the systems they use, can be very effective at reducing reoffending, and in my experience the best ways to achieve change is through the accurate assessment of offenders and the correct implementation of appropriate interventions. However, this can be tricky to get right, so with this in mind I will highlight some of the obstacles the practitioner may face and then share some ideas on how to overcome them.

In writing this chapter and book I do not mean to suggest that the ideas expressed are solely for those working within the YOS or Probation Service. Readers who are not in the Probation or YOS professions will hopefully find value in the ideas, exercises and strategies expressed, and prove able to apply them to their own practice - no matter what organisation they work in.

The Rehabilitative Path of the Offender

Often, people who have been arrested, sentenced or placed on bail by the courts will at some point enter into the jurisdiction (in one way or another) of the Probation Service or YOS. Therefore I will start by looking at the role of the Probation Service and YOS with regards to addressing offending behaviour.

When an individual who commits a crime appears at court, the court often requests a report from the Probation Service or YOS. The function of these reports is to assist magistrates or judges with possible sentences and disposals prior to sentencing. In order to do this, a number of areas are looked at. These can include:

- An assessment and analysis of the offending individual's viewpoint with regards to the offence
- Potential victim issues
- The offender's background and current circumstances
- An assessment of the risk of serious harm that the individual poses to others, including themselves

On occasion, the above reports may be verbal reports. This is where, after a brief interview with the offender, a professional will present their findings to the court. These are formally known as Oral Reports and will usually be presented by a member of the YOS or Probation Service.

In some cases, usually more complex ones, more comprehensive written reports will be requested, and these are known in both the YOS and Probation Service as Pre-Sentence Reports (PSRs). The PSR will look at a number of different areas – not just the areas bulleted above – and include an assessment into the likelihood of re-conviction, and the likelihood of re-offending.

Once an offender's assessment is made, the reports will conclude by offering the courts a suggestion on possible sentencing disposals that the offender is deemed 'suitable for'. In order for the practitioner to assess sentencing options in the PSR, a number of further factors are looked at. These factors include:

- Directions from the courts (here the courts state the seriousness of the offence and sometimes what they feel is an appropriate disposal or length of sentence)
- Magistrates Sentencing Guidelines (both the Probation Service and YOS use these)
- Local availability of resources (these are different in different areas)
- The dynamic and static features of the offender's behaviour (discussed later)
- Local policies

Let's move things along and assume an offending individual has been sentenced or directed by the courts to a disposal which involves some element of Probation or YOS oversight. The purpose of this being (hypothetically) to rehabilitate and address specific offending behaviour.

However, before we move on, I feel that it is important to explain that not all sentences directed by the courts are intended to have a purpose of rehabilitation. Some directions from the court may solely involve a punitive element or a combination of directions. The directions from the courts follow five main purposes. These are:

- A proposal focusing on Punishment
- A proposal focusing on Reduction in crime
- A proposal focusing on Reform and Rehabilitation
- A proposal focusing on Reparation
- A proposal focusing on Public Protection

As discussed above, my goal here is to focus on rehabilitation as this element is where probation officers spend a lot of time with their clients, but I will also touch on reform, as well as punishment which will be mainly discussed in the final chapters. Discussing the other directions is not within the remit of this book.

When considering the rehabilitation side of sentencing - a practitioner will look at the 'needs' an individual has. These 'needs' are known as criminogenic needs. Criminogenic needs can be thought of as: *specific factors that relate to that individual's offending behaviour* and are different to what we might view as generic or welfare needs. Welfare needs or generic needs tend to be *all the factors or problems that the individual has, that are not related to their offending behaviour*.

All needs, criminogenic or not, vary according to the individual and we need to know the differences between welfare and criminogenic factors. This is because, in part, one of the aims of the CJS is to reduce reoffending, not to solve the client's day-to-day problems. So, as such, the practitioner needs to focus all their efforts on specifics rather than looking at peripheral problems. Can you imagine how long it would take to address all somebody's day-to-day problems? More on criminogenic needs later!

Following the assessment of the offender by the practitioner, the courts can impose a number of possible rehabilitative interventions known as 'requirements'. The most pertinent ones to this book are:

- *Probation or YOS Supervision* (one-to-one and group sessions). The meaning of supervision is not only to address offending behaviour on a one-to-one basis but it can also be used to restrict that individual's liberty as a form of punishment, monitor their behaviour, and assist that individual with further complex needs (such as accommodation, employment and education issues).

- *Specified Activities* (an activity as defined by the practitioner). An example of specified activities would be activities or structured work to address a particular need such as, but not exclusively limited to, substance misuse. They are developed, reviewed, and monitored on a local basis. A specified activity can also be group work or one-to-one work.

- *Programmes* (group or individual). A programme is specially designed or structured work, delivered within a group or individual setting, aimed at addressing singular or multiple problematic behaviours. Additionally, programmes are evidence based and reviewed on a national basis, while specified activities are more locally appropriate.

Once a client has been sentenced to a disposal such as the above - the probation officer or YOS case manager can then look to start undertaking specific work that promotes change. However, before this, the practitioner needs to ensure that they get the assessment of the offender correct, so let's look at assessments in some detail.

Making High Quality Assessments

Pre-Sentence Reports (PSRs) are informed by risk assessments, and the primary tool the Probation Service uses to assess the risk that an individual poses is what is known as an Offender Assessment System (OASys), whilst the YOS uses an ASSET assessment (note that ASSET is not an acronym but a name). Then, once these risk assessments have been completed on a computer system, the system actually generates the reports for practitioners.

To acquire the information required to complete the risk assessments, the practitioner will need to obtain information from a number of sources to ensure that their risk assessment is well informed. The sources of information will always include an interview with the client to obtain a first-hand account of how they perceive their circumstances. Other sources of information can include:

- Screening questionnaires
- Information from other voluntary agencies
- Police intelligence
- Discussions with family members
- Social Care intelligence
- Local authority records

During the OASys and ASSET assessments a number of factors are assessed in detail and these are the aforementioned 'criminogenic needs' (also known as dynamic factors). To be more specific, the criminogenic needs assessed by the professional are:

- Offence analysis (the Who, When, What, Why, and How)
- The offender's Education and Employment status
- The offender's Relationships (both family and intimate)
- Finances (looking at income, money management, etc.)
- Thinking and Behaviour (such as acting impulsively and problem solving)
- Substance Misuse (drugs and alcohol)
- Emotional Wellbeing (depression, self-harm, etc.)
- General Attitudes (towards probation, life, crime etc.)
- General Health (any significant physical problems that affect the offender)

After assessing all of the criminogenic factors, the practitioner will need to make a judgement of the risk of serious harm an individual poses to others and themselves. The practitioner will also need to identify the likelihood of that individual reoffending.

This judgement, however, will always have to be based on the *evidence* a practitioner finds. A practitioner cannot or should not make sweeping generalised comments into the risk of serious harm or anything to do with risk assessment. So, for example, when looking at criminogenic needs, if someone has been assessed as having a particular problem with their thinking and behaviour, then the practitioner will need to explain exactly what parts of their thinking and behaviour is a problem. An example of a well formed sentence explaining a criminogenic need could be:

"David acts impulsively when in confrontational situations and under the influence of alcohol. This has been demonstrated by his current offences and previous convictions."

When undertaking risk assessments, the practitioner should always look for the links between any of the factors identified above and offending. A practitioner will also need to link these factors to any risk of serious harm (if they feel them to be associated). In order to do this, the practitioner will need to use their professional judgement and understanding of current research – more of which will be covered later.

Chapter 1

As mentioned earlier, when a practitioner undertakes an analysis for assessment, he or she should always use *evidence based* decision making and examples to back up their thinking. So, for example, for a more holistic report, the incorporation of assessments from other professionals (such as mental health assessors) should be included. These can often be difficult to obtain, and are usually only obtained if requested by the Probation Service, the YOS, or the courts.

The process of considering dynamic features or criminogenic needs is called making a clinical assessment. In addition to making these clinical assessments, the OASys and ASSET assessments will also incorporate an element of statistical calculation. These statistical tools are known as *actuarial tools*.

One of the tools the Probation Service uses is a tool known as the Offender Group Reconviction Scale (OGRS). This highly useful tool generates a statistical likelihood, in numerical form, of the probability that an individual with 'a similar offending history' will be re-convicted within twelve months, and also in two years. The OGRS assessment is calculated by taking into account what's known as 'static factors'. These are factors that are fact. The static factors used to calculate OGRS are:

- Offence type
- Number of previous court appearances
- Age of first conviction
- Current age
- Date of the current offence (the current offence is sometimes referred to as the index offence)

OGRSs, in my experience, are very useful but it is important to recognise their limitations. OGRSs generate a prediction of re-conviction which has used a historical sample group of white male offenders during a specific period of time. This in my mind raises a few questions, such as: *"what relevance does this have to, let's say, a black female offender?"*

In my opinion, it is not possible to compare a group of white male offenders and female offenders. Moreover, how can we use this tool with offenders who suffer from mental health problems? Surely the complex needs of those with mental health problems cannot realistically be stereotyped in the same manner? An example could be a female offender, suffering from Attention Deficit Hyperactivity Disorder (ADHD) who is prone to acting impulsively when intoxicated. Simplistically, the calculated OGRS value of a likelihood of re-conviction cannot be valid. Similarly, the ASSET assessment generates a statistical figure which predicts the likelihood of re-offending (notice not re-conviction) from its own sample group. Again the same issues, as described above, are present.

Critically, in my experience, the practitioner can sometimes take these scores at face value rather than really analysing them. I have seen some practitioners simply accept the figures as fact rather than deliberating upon them before indicating whether they concur or not. To help question the interpretation of statistically generated figures, I always ask myself the following questions:

- Do I agree with the actuarial tools used? If not, explain why!

- Is this offending behaviour part of an *emerging* pattern of offending behaviour?

- Is this offence more serious than their last?

- Is this offence part of an *established* pattern of offending?

Asking these questions helps to provide a critical assessment of the actuarial tools used, such as OGRS, and it is worth remarking how the assessment of any offender should use a combination of actuarial and clinical tools. By using different tool types practitioners are able to make more holistic assessments.

To recap: with every offender, risk assessment tools should work in conjunction with each other, even with those offenders who do not tally with specific research groups. However, the results of these assessment tools should only be seen as skeleton structures. Professional judgment, evidence based reasoning, and critical analysis is needed for a fuller report.

What is Risk?

In this chapter, I have loosely mentioned risk and the risk of serious harm. But what does this actually mean? And why is knowing about risk important?

Before I answer this, it is important that I point out how risk assessments used by the Probation Service and YOS seek to identify clearly: the risk of serious harm an individual poses, the relevant criminogenic needs for that client, and the likelihood of an offender reoffending. This is important for not only sentencing, but for implementing interventions and effectively managing cases. This has been briefly explored earlier. So what is risk and risk of serious harm?

Risk can be defined as:

"The probability that a particular adverse event occurs during a stated period of time, or results from a particular challenge." (Report of a Royal Society Study Group 1992 cited in Kemshall 1997)

And serious harm means:

"Death or serious personal injury, whether physical or psychological that is difficult or impossible to recover from." (S.s 224-225 CJA03)

Understanding the differences between these definitions is critical for completing risk assessments as it is easy to get confused.

Notice that risk talks about the probability of something happening. In my mind, this relates directly to knowing what triggers, controls, and influences the criminogenic needs discussed earlier. Then, serious harm refers to the actual harm that could happen if one of those criminogenic needs is triggered. This includes both psychological and physical damage.

By knowing what influences the risk of serious harm an individual poses, and what the level is, we can seek to control it and put in place the correct interventions. Additionally, by knowing the level we will know what level of intensity we will need to work at with that client. The levels of risk of harm are as follows:

- Low risk of serious harm
- Medium risk of serious harm
- High risk of serious harm
- Very High risk of serious harm

Now, each level has its own definition, but this will not be discussed here. Just know that the level of harm generally refers predominately to the probability of serious harm occurring, under what conditions it will happen, and the damage it will cause.

Once the practitioner knows what level and type of risk an individual poses. We need to consider the following questions in order to protect the public and reduce reoffending:

- What is the risk specifically?
- Who is at risk specifically from the offender?
- What signs demonstrate an increase in risk?
- What factors reduce the risk?

This is all part of the risk assessment process in the OASys and ASSET tools. The courts will also need to know this at the PSR stage.

When considering these questions, you must first take each individual case on its own merits and reflect on the *internal* and *external* elements *or controls* that relate to the offender's behaviour.

One way to define internal controls is: *positive and negative thought processes that either increase or decrease the likelihood of an individual acting in an offending behavioural manner.* So, for example, the practitioner will need to consider answering the following questions (to name but a few): Does the offender have good coping strategies? Does the offender show remorse? Does the offender take responsibility?

One way to define external controls is: *positive and negative factors, that are around the offender, that either increase of decrease the likelihood of them acting in an offending manner to cause harm.* For example, does the offender have a supportive family, suitable accommodation, or even regular and stable employment? All these factors can have some impact on risk levels and the right interventions. Note here that much of the research that has looked into common internal and external controls, alongside identifying criminogenic needs and appropriate interventions, are discussed throughout the forthcoming chapters.

Enhancing Risk Assessments

Earlier in this chapter, I wrote about the importance of the practitioner understanding current research and theory and, at the time of writing this book, there seems to be a professional emphasis on this very point - a push on incorporating theory and current research findings into the assessments of offenders. In my experience, this is highly useful and an excellent way to support and give evidence to opinions.

There are numerous theories and research findings that can be utilised by the practitioner, many of which can be made available by the organisation a practitioner works in. But having so much choice means that things can become confusing. So to simplify the matter, rather than explaining all the different theories, I have cherry picked some of what I think are the best and most useful theories and research and incorporated them into the relevant chapters in this book. Therefore, to enhance your risk assessments further, go to the relevant chapters in this book depending on your need, and apply the theories to your risk assessments as appropriate.

Other Considerations for Risk Assessments

Here are a few additional points I would like the reader to consider regarding the use of risk assessments.

When an OASys or ASSET risk assessment is completed, they might be used to inform a number of other different reports. These other reports include: prison reports, reports to Social Care, and sometimes they are used to form part of a referral to other professional bodies. The purpose of risk assessments is to provide a current and up-to-date risk appraisal of an individual - information that these organisations need.

Given that both the Probation Service and YOS are required by the government to provide consistency in approach throughout the country, OASys and ASSET assessments are 'governed' by what is known as *National Minimum Standards*. National Minimum Standards are guidelines outlining when, and how often, assessments should be completed. Typically, they will indicate when an individual should be assessed and reassessed. At the time of writing, best practice suggests assessments should be carried out at the beginning of a sentence, at regular intervals during the course of the sentence, at the end, and whenever there is a significant change in circumstances which affects risk levels.

These reviews can be, and have been, 'cash linked targets' so that services can demonstrate accountability and effectiveness. Needless to say, linking assessments with targets was not the original intention behind the assessment process. The original intention was simply to provide an accurate and defensible risk assessment of the individual being assessed to ensure a suitable imposition of disposals.

National Standards often change, and this can have a significant impact on how the practitioner effectively evaluates risk. An example of bad practice could be a practitioner rushing to make an assessment and producing a flawed assessment to ensure targets are met. The implications of this alone can have a major effect on the rights of an offender. However, I am only stressing that this is *possible* and do not suggest that this is being done routinely.

All Probation and YOS assessments inform a plan of change for the offender known as a *sentence plan*. It is therefore vital to make the assessment of the offender as accurate as you can.

Know Yourself to Make a Great Assessment

When reading the previous section on assessments, it is easy to be critical of the processes and systems involved. But do not feel despondent. In my view, it is only through reflection and sharing knowledge than we can truly grow as practitioners and produce high quality assessments. So here are just two of the questions that I have reflected upon in my own practice.

Can objectivity really be achieved? And does being able to empathise with an individual through their struggle really provide an accurate insight into them and thus a valid assessment?

I would argue – yes – objectivity can be achieved and – yes – you can still provide a valid assessment by ensuring you use professional and evidence based decision making. This will depend hugely on the practitioner asking the right questions in the correct manner, and recording the information they receive accurately. In my experience, one thing that really helps a practitioner maintain objectivity is *know yourself*.

Reflect on your past experiences a little as I believe (and Cognitive Behavioural Therapy confirms this) that our past experiences affect the way we act now. They influence our opinions about ourselves, how we see others, and how we see the world. Recognise when you may, or may not, become affected by a specific topic and consciously remain critical of yourself in the way you receive information. We shall cover this some more in later chapters. *Knowing yourself* will enable you to carry out your role better!

The reason assessments are discussed before we look at specific strategies for addressing offending behaviour is that it is vital to have two basic fundamentals covered before you start working with offenders. Firstly you need as accurate an assessment as possible of an individual's needs, and secondly you need a positive working relationship with that person. Relationships will be discussed in the next chapter.

Beginning to Plan Interventions to Start Change

For the purpose of keeping things simple, I will hypothetically assume that the practitioner, or whoever is making an assessment of an individual, has got the risk assessment as accurate as possible. It is, of course, almost impossible to get it one hundred percent correct!

The practitioner now has to put in place a more detailed sentence plan that meshes with the sentence imposed by the court. Prior to this, the practitioner would have given the courts an idea of what this may be (in brief) in the PSR. The more detailed plan is also influenced by the level of risk that the individual poses and the plan itself is heavily influenced by how much contact the practitioner has with the offender.

Both the Probation Service and YOS have different methods of calculating the number of sessions an individual is required to attend. The Probation Service's method is based around a risk of 'serious harm' that an individual poses, and thus the higher the risk - the higher the number of contacts. For example, an individual who is deemed a *high risk of harm* could attend probation supervision on a minimum of a weekly basis for a certain period of time. Whereas those identified as low risk of harm can be seen as little as once a quarter.

The YOS, on the other hand, currently uses what is known as a *scaled approach* and it is based on two elements: the risk of harm the individual poses, and (importantly) the likelihood of re-offending. A young person, for example, may hold a high likelihood of re-offending but represent a low risk of harm to the public. This might be a shoplifter who commits many offences on a daily basis but who does not represent a serious risk of physical or emotional damage to the public. But this individual may have just as many contacts as a person who is deemed a high risk of harm, because of the frequency of their offending behaviour.

It is worth noting that both methods of calculating the number of appointments, despite their complexities, are in response (one way or another) to the level of risk a client represents, or a likelihood of re-offending.

Being responsive to this form of 'need' is a fundamental principle which I feel should be followed by anyone addressing offending behaviour. In my view contacts should be determined in this way:

The higher the risk of serious harm posed, or the higher the likelihood of re-offending someone poses, the more contacts you should have with this person.

The Basics of a Good Sentence Plan

Now, regardless of the professional organisation, it is my view that anyone who is addressing offending behaviour must look at the client as an *individual* and look at the *specific* factors related to that person's offending. Both the Probation Service and YOS do this and prepare the aforementioned sentence plan. Then, in one form or another, the plan is put down on paper and presented to the offender.

When developing a sentence plan, a negotiation takes place between the offender and the practitioner with regards to the objectives that need to be achieved to reduce the risk of the client re-offending or posing a risk to others. This can sometimes be a very difficult process to get the offender to engage in but if the sentence plan is 'sold' well - the client, in my experience, will give it a go.

One way to 'sell' the sentence plan to the offender is by building a relationship with the client and empowering them to make changes through reflection and goal setting (explored in depth in the next chapter). When getting the client to give the sentence plan a go, it is important that any goals or targets are made SMART targets. SMART concepts have been around for some time, but are very effective. SMART is:

- Specific (the goal is clear, it is unambiguous)
- Measurable (progress towards the goal can be evaluated and quantified)
- Attainable (the goal is achievable even if it is a stretch case)
- Realistic (the goal matters, it is relevant to what is being sought overall)
- Time bound (goals exist within a time frame, meaning that target dates are agreed)

The use of SMART goals is a common cognitive behavioural strategy and a very useful one at that. An example of one in relation to ensuring a client attends his appointments (this can be a huge task for some clients) could be:

"I will attend all sessions, on time, as required, over the next sixteen weeks."

For those with highly complex needs, I would suggest that you actually start with simple targets (such as the example above) and then build up from there. For some clients, the action of actually getting to appointments can be a huge motivational achievement.

Once you have the client engaged (discussed in the next chapter) it is important to then focus on the goals that address offending behaviour. For example, if you need to monitor an offender's alcohol misuse, as it is linked to risk, then a goal could be:

"I will complete a drink/drug diary over the next week."

In my experience, goal setting is one of the most important aspects of planning a successful rehabilitation of any type. Do it right and it can be highly effective for successful treatment. Do it wrong, and it can be detrimental and reinforce an individual's negative self-image. It can also reinforce the individual's belief that the sanctions of the courts, Probation Service, or YOS have no meaning or are simply punitive in nature, thereby reinforcing their offending behaviour. For example, one way to make sure that a depressive stays depressed is to ensure that they set themselves unrealistic goals and targets which reinforce negative self-beliefs so that they 'fail to live up to their own standard and goals'.

When goal setting, here are two good tips to consider. Firstly, one should review the goal (or goals) regularly and break any big task into smaller manageable steps. Remember to give praise for positive progression. Next, discussing the obstacles to achieving goals is of equal importance to actually achieving the goals themselves. During the discussion, it is critical to ensure that a failure to achieve a desired goal does not affect an individual's self-esteem as this could lead to them re-offending or potentially harming themselves or others. Therefore, one way to achieve this is to explain to the client that setbacks are normal and part of life. We simply need to look at ways to overcome them for the future.

Of course you cannot plan for everything, but I would argue that you should be able to predict a few circumstances that could get in the way of goals. Remember to *sell the idea* that an individual should be prepared for setbacks by planning for them.

More on Obstacles to Success

More frequently than not in professions such as the Probation Service and YOS, you come across individuals who were assessed during court proceedings as being motivated to change, who then completely shift in their attitude after sentencing. It appears to the observer that they 'played the game'. They demonstrated remorse for their behaviour before: they cried, they showed insight into their problems, and were highly motivated to change. They may even have told the courts and the practitioner everything that they wanted to hear. Now, they just want to 'get it done', do not care about their problems, and are in denial about many of the problems they once had insight into. Here is an example of how this has happened to me with a client in my own practice.

> During a Pre-Sentence Report interview Jo told me that he was ashamed of his behaviour and for hitting the victim. Jo stated that he would do anything to take back what he did and was willing to stop consuming the levels of alcohol he drank prior to the offence.
>
> Following the imposition of a community based penalty (probation supervision), Jo told me during our first appointment: "I don't really care about what I did, and I won't stop using alcohol because I like it."

This is not always the case, of course, and some individuals who pass through the Criminal Justice System continue to be motivated. I am simply demonstrating one of the frequent and frustrating issues with this complex behaviour.

Looking at Jo and individuals who shift in attitude, the practitioner is now faced with several dilemmas, possible actions, and questions. These are:

- Did they get the assessment right before sentencing?
- Do they take this order back to court if they can?
- Do they try to work with this individual who is pre-contemplative at best, with regards to their behaviour?

More often than not, the practitioner will attempt to work with an individual pending no significant changes in risk or circumstances. Unfortunately, and possibly unsurprisingly, 'offenders lie' and that is just how it is. Do not take it personally. You most likely did get the assessment right based on the information you obtained.

Tip: When you feel new information from the offender is significant and impacts the risk of serious harm then you should always update and review your risk assessments.

So the question now is even if they have lied, will they still benefit from the intervention you proposed to the court, and what is the best way to engage with that client to get the best possible outcome?

In chapter two, we shall look at ways to work with this resistance, but in the meantime, you should always look to the client to see where they could obtain some form of motivation to change. For example, have they got a family? Is the family proud of the client's behaviour? Does the client have children? Do they want to be there for their children? And so on. In my experience, unless an offender has nothing to lose (sometimes they might say this but do not mean it) there is always some source of external motivation that can be utilised. You just need to find it. In some cases, I have used "Do this for your children," for months until clients started to see they *could* change and built up their own internal motivation.

To conclude this section - when working with demotivated offenders, always ensure that you plan your sessions to cover specific problems *related to the individual.* By undertaking exercises that have little or no relevance to the offender (demotivated or not) they can lose concentration and disengage.

Summary

In this chapter, we explored in brief what I called 'the rehabilitative path' an offender can take before and after being sentenced by the courts for a criminal offence. What we saw here, is that the courts ultimately determine the sentence that an offender receives, but they are usually equipped with information and guidance from the Probation and Youth Offending Services.

We also saw that the courts can impose many different types of disposals. Some of these disposals may not be aimed at rehabilitation for the offender. On occasion, the court's main focus can be (especially for adults) disposals that promote public protection and even ones that simply punish. However, more and more, I have seen the courts determine that rudimentary punishment is not working in the fight to reduce crime, but rehabilitation can and does have an effect.

When practitioners make assessments that begin to address offending behaviour - they have a huge level of responsibility to get their assessment as accurate as possible. This is because assessments not only affect the offender but also possibly the victim, the community, the offender's family, the victim's family, and so on.

In this chapter, we explored some of the ideas and strategies that help ensure that the practitioner gets the assessment of the offender spot on. Additionally we looked at how to enhance these risk assessments by incorporating theory and research to make defensible decisions.

To facilitate effective change in any individual, it is my view that a practitioner must accurately assess the offender *from the onset.* By doing this, the professional is able to understand the factors linked to their behaviour and, as such, is able to plan effectively in how to reduce the risk that offender poses. In order to plan for effective change, the *quality* of the sentence plan is highly important. By using SMART goal setting as the basis for all targets for the offender, a practitioner can improve the outcome they desire. Trust me, it really does work!

As we move through the upcoming chapters, keep in mind the points we have discussed in this chapter. Always seek to consider how to apply SMART goal setting and evidence-based decision making. Also make sure you use as many sources of information as possible. *Never assume anything* if you want to make a holistic assessment.

Chapter 1

In the next chapter, we will look at how to engage with an offender after sentencing. This can be extremely difficult at times and you will need to know the ways of working around resistance. Let's move on, and see how you can do this!

2
The Working Relationship

In my experience, one of the most important factors when addressing offending behaviour is being able to establish an *effective working relationship* with the client. This idea has been of fluctuating significance throughout the history of both the Probation Service and Youth Offending Service (YOS). For example, the work of the Probation Service has previously been conceptualised by the term "advise, assist and befriend" but more recently there has been a heightened focus on enforcement as a means to evidence the increasing agenda of public protection. The current agenda, at the time of writing, has a heavy focus on incorporating both public protection and an offender centred approach.

Despite the ever-changing agenda of the Probation Service and YOS (which is ultimately controlled by the government) I will look at why the relationship between the practitioner and client is so important, and why it should always remain at the forefront of any practitioner's contacts with the offender.

To ensure the path of the offender is kept in sequence with chapter one, I will describe the starting point of when a practitioner comes into contact with an offender following sentencing. From here, I will begin to explore the foundations that the working relationship should be built on. In doing so, we shall begin to discover and understand the complex dynamics of any relationship, and how they can subsequently affect the initial stages of interventions.

Following this, I will discuss why the issue of the working relationship is so vital and shall draw upon relevant research and my own experience. Here you will find a number of tips on how to improve relationships with offenders.

When reading this chapter, you will see that it is not just about how to manage troubled relationships with offenders, rather it explores some of the most powerful basic strategies used to engage with offenders holding all levels of motivation. I will put forward case studies and examples explaining how to implement these skills. Remember, these case studies are not clients' real names, but they are real cases.

A Shaky Start for Any Relationship

A client in the current Criminal Justice System (CJS) will usually become involved with the Probation Service or YOS when they have been convicted of an offence (unless it is through preventative measures). Being convicted of an offence can happen in one of two ways, either through pleading guilty, or being found guilty at trial. Both processes can pose problems and present a shaky basis for any working relationship.

The path of pleading guilty

Let's suppose that the offender has pleaded guilty. Before the practitioner meets with the offender, it is pertinent for them to think about the offender's motivation for pleading guilty. Was it out of remorse? Was it done to secure a lesser sentence? Was it because the offender wanted to change? Or was it because of some loyalty to a criminal subculture?

Often, in my experience, it can be a combination of all or some of these factors. But what the reader should be aware of is that if an offender pleads guilty at court, then the sentence they receive will usually be reduced substantially. Offenders seem to recognise this well. So ask yourself - how does the path of pleading guilty affect the relationship building process?

The path of guilt after trial

Despite the various reasons for pleading guilty, let us assume that an individual has been found guilty at trial. This does not now mean that the individual necessarily accepts their guilt or even that they take any responsibility for the offence. It also does not mean that they feel they need to change their ways. In some cases, an offender will continue to proclaim that there has been a miscarriage of justice and that the 'system has got it wrong'.

After sentencing, the offender has the right to appeal, but until the appeal has been resolved they are managed by the Probation Service and YOS on the basis of having been found guilty. On the flip side, the individual at court will sometimes accept their guilt passively. But regardless of how this verdict is achieved, the relationship between the practitioner and the client is hugely important as in each circumstance there are different obstacles to working together.

In my mind, what makes the Probation Service and YOS so unique is that they would appear to be two of the few organisations in the world that work with *involuntary* clients for rehabilitation. My meaning of involuntary clients being that offenders will often not feel that they have to change, or even want to, as they are directed to do so by the courts. This is why the role of addressing offending behaviour can be so complex.

It is worth noting here that adding to the complexity of the working relationship, and in addition to the legal processes, is the need for the practitioner to remember that offenders come into contact with the Probation Service and YOS with a whole range of distinctive *previous experiences* of the Criminal Justice System. They also have a wide array of different (and often complex) life experiences - all of which will impact on the working relationship.

Why is the Relationship Important

Forming an effective working relationship with a client can be very effective in helping the offender to move away from offending behaviour and taking a different path. Once a relationship is formed, an offender begins to trust your judgement as a professional and in some ways begins to develop a sense of moral obligation to you. As such, they do not want to let you, the practitioner, down. I would argue that although this is external motivation and not conducive to long term change, it can be considered (at the very least) a good start. This is because, ultimately, you will need to get the client into your sessions so that you can begin to work with them and start to build their own internal motivation. This is discussed later in the chapter, but until then, I would like you to reflect on the issue of trust. Ask yourself the following question: how can you realistically facilitate any kind of change in a client (unwilling or willing) without their respect or, at the very least, their trust?

In order to empower the offender to make changes, most of the practitioner's tools are based around using the skills of Cognitive Behaviour Therapy (CBT). This can be life changing for some people.

However, in my experience, CBT has a problem (despite the tactics around some of these issues discussed later) when used on the front line with unmotivated offenders. I would argue that because it is based on many seemingly 'common sense' principles, it relies heavily on the motivation of the offender to participate in structured work such as programmes. For example, an offender may be asked to complete written tasks at home – so the client must also trust in you, and the material, to be willing and actively complete it. See why this sense of moral obligation is important now?

Should a sense of moral obligation not be present, one of the practitioner's tasks is to try to gain the trust of the offender by simply discussing their day-to-day problems and then seeking to address offending behaviour during these one-to-one sessions.

Sometimes, if a practitioner is unable to undertake CBT with a client in the early stages of their contact, the practitioner may feel as though they are not doing their job correctly. However, by beginning to talk to the client about their day-to-day problems you are creating the beginnings of the working relationship, so you should not be disillusioned. I have found that by talking about people's problems with them you *begin* to gain their trust. Once you gain the trust of the offender, you can then encourage them to participate in structured work willingly.

What Kind of Relationship Do We Want?

Once we recognise that building an effective working relationship is beneficial for change, we need to consider what we mean by effective working relationship. So here, it is important for me to outline how I feel this should be defined. The best way I can do this is by looking at what we are trying to achieve with the offender, therefore:

An effective working relationship is not trying to befriend an offender, it is a relationship where we are able to create a sense of discontent about their current behaviour and yet support them to make better decisions and take a new pro-social path.

When thinking about the type of relationship we are trying to form, it is important that offenders realise how all change involves some element of loss. This loss could be in a number of different ways such as losing negative friends, losing or changing their current way of life, or losing their current way of thinking. It is also important that professionals acknowledge that there is a positive side to offending for the offender. Without us openly doing this, both parties will not feel as though they can take the perspective of the other and there you have it - another barrier!

When an offender feels as though you (the professional) cannot take their perspective, this can be seen as another reason why change for them will be hard. If the practitioner does not address this, it can make the atmosphere very uncomfortable for offenders. Even for practitioners, when they realise that they cannot take the offender's perspective, such an environment can feel uncomfortable. So, practitioners have to remember how important perspective is.

More on Gaining Trust

Generally, I believe (and I hope I am not being naive) that all practitioners who enter professions such as the Probation Service or YOS, do so because they want to make a difference. This means that the practitioner wants to stop (or reduce) people offending and they want to help offenders change their lives for the better. To do this, I would state that the practitioner will need some level of trust and respect *from their client*. This is because the client will need to talk about their thoughts, feelings, and behaviours – all of which are *essential* for undertaking CBT.

Talking about feelings, thoughts and behaviours can be a massive 'ask' for an offender or anyone for that matter. Furthermore, when getting the offender to express themselves, matters may be further complicated by the fact that many people may have broken their trust previously. The offender may even fear that if they do open up, they might get into more trouble than they are already in. This relates specifically to information that the offender may feel will impact on the management of their case. As practitioners, we have an obligation to share information with any other relevant agency should disclosure influence an increase in risk.

Based on this, it is paramount that clear boundaries are set at the beginning of an intervention. Practitioners should clearly state *what* and *when* information will be shared. By explaining this, we show the limitations of how we will work. The offender needs to know that although we will work within the boundaries of data protection we will not 'keep secrets' especially ones which could have a significant impact on others. Especially children, the public, or themselves! So, for example, if we feel a child is at risk, then we should immediately contact Social Care.

When professionals make referrals to agencies such as Social Care, these actions can evoke huge negative reactions from the offender. However, if the practitioner feels a child is at risk, a referral is essential and the practitioner should explain to the offender why they have taken this action. They should also explain that they (as the professional) will still be - in a professional capacity anyway- working alongside the offender no matter what the outcome. By doing this, and by being there for clients through the 'ups and downs' of their life as a consistent figure, we help build trust.

So, when we try to establish trust with these offenders, it is vital to consider their life encounters. They may have had a whole range of different and negative life experiences, including various relationship let-downs (both personal and professional). The implication of this for the practitioner is that the offender may struggle with opening up, be overly defensive, or even prove distrustful of you. So try to explore these previous encounters and look at ways to overcome problems. One way to help establish trust is by being consistent; this can be as simple as fixing appointments with the offender at the same agreed time each week. You would be surprised at how important consistency is for many clients in this way!

ou are able to explore the issue of trust with your offenders, you will probably see they have developed rigid beliefs from their past experiences. Some examples of these come in the form of individualistic moral codes such as: "I do not trust anyone especially professionals," or "Do not talk to anyone about your problems as you will always be let down." In order to break this cycle, I have found that the consistency discussed above and the willingness of the practitioner to explore these codes is the key. If you say you are going to do something for a client, then do it! This also applies to my earlier point of the offender attending appointments on time. If an offender does this, then so should we! Remember, by providing an offender with a consistent and reliable figure, they should begin to trust you and the negative moral codes they expressed before will begin to be broken down.

To help the practitioner explore moral codes, here is one great method you could use. I have found this to work especially well with young offenders. I like to call it the *My World Poster* and it is an exercise that is also a bit of fun.

My World Poster

Step 1. Ask the client to draw themselves in the middle of a piece of flip chart paper. They can draw themselves in as little or as much detail as they feel necessary. For example, a smiley face or stick person will suffice. Feel free to have some fun with this and use different colours.

Step 2. Next, ask the client to think about who is most important to them. Then draw lines coming out of the figure and write down the names or initials of those important people. Write as many as you can.

Step 3. Now ask the client what these people *mean* to them. Write the answers down next to the names.

Step 4. Next, ask the client to draw more lines coming out of 'them' (i.e. the smiley face) and write down any strong beliefs that they have about life topics such as religion, friends, politics and more.

Step 5. Now ask them to write (as the title of the poster) a motto or saying that they think is pertinent to their life.

And there you have it; you have begun to explore their world and moral codes!

What is the Evidence for Trust Being Vital?

When looking into the world of academia, there is increasing supporting evidence for the status of working relationships being an important factor in reducing crime. Watson (2003) as cited in Burnett and McNeil (2005) suggests that: "*it is the development of a working alliance, a process of give and take, and the development of trust and moral obligation that is important for the rehabilitation of offenders.*" From a common sense perspective, this is difficult to argue against: how can a client talk to you without trust and the feeling that they are being listened to?

An example of how the working relationship is important can be seen within my own professional practice and the case study of Paul.

Paul was a 67 year old, and sentenced to a 12 month Community Order with one-to-one supervision for the offence of Driving Under the Influence of Alcohol. There was a significant age difference, with him being older than me, and an immediate barrier arose in his eyes.

In order to achieve a working relationship with Paul, I spoke to him about how *I trusted* that he would *co-operate* and *take ownership* of this court imposed order.

The purpose of this was for me, as a practitioner, to use the foundations of a trust based relationship so that I could, and I quote from Watson (2003): "*get the offender around to our way of thinking*" cited in Burnett and McNeil (2005). This in my mind could be achieved by giving Paul a sense of ownership and responsibility.

The strategy worked well, and Paul saw out the Community Order with no significant issues.

It is important to note that the above strategy may not work for everyone. But in the case of Paul, *trust* helped him to develop a sense of moral obligation through a process of 'give and take'. I explained to him that if he did not attend his appointments, then he should be fully aware that warning letters would be sent to him and that ultimately everything was under his control.

Rex (1999) cited in Burnett and McNeil (2005) elaborates on such methods by commenting on her own research which concluded that offenders appreciate the efforts of their supervising officers and make an effort on their behalf in order not to let them down.

In my own practice, I have found that one way a practitioner can ensure clients begin to achieve this moral obligation and a trusting relationship, is by the practitioner being truly interested in their cases and helping their clients change. I believe that the offender can pick up on real or genuine interest naturally.

To help further in building moral obligation and an effective working relationship, the practitioner needs to make sure that they do their research on each case and gets as much knowledge as they can on each offender.

To be specific, the practitioner should conduct research in the following areas before the first meeting:

- Information about the most recent offence

- History of offending behaviour and general background

- Work undertaken with any other agency

- Work undertaken previously with your service

By doing this research, I feel that you communicate to the offender that you have taken the time to learn about them, that you are well prepared, and ready to help them make a difference in their life. Never go into a session with an offender without any knowledge of them at all. This can be dangerous!

The Basic Skills for Relationship Building

At the root of any working relationship, I believe, a professional must be passionate and want to help the client in front of them. The moment a practitioner stops feeling this way or begins to feel that an offender has no chance at all of change - I would suggest they take a break and 're-group'.

Of course you cannot change everyone but I would argue that you can still assist with elements of any client's behaviour. To help you further, I want to offer you the following underlying belief that I feel is critical for any practitioner. Truly believing this statement could assist you in maintaining the motivation to work with clients in difficult times as it has on occasion helped me:

Change for anyone is difficult, and desistance from crime should always be seen as a slow 'up and down' process for an individual. Your job is to stick by them, and decrease the frequency of offending until you can get it to stop, where possible.

Earlier in the chapter, I wrote how the Probation Service and YOS are two of the few organisations in the world that work with involuntary clients. When a practitioner is able to recognise how motivated someone is to change, it significantly helps the working relationship. This is because, once we know how motivated someone is, we can wor their *particular level* and then move them forward. In my experience, if we do not at the offender's level, then the offender often becomes frustrated and can disengage with us. Pinpointing someone's level of motivation will be discussed shortly but for now let's consider a motivated individual to be someone who is *ready, willing and able*.

To build up an effective working relationship, and build up an offender's level of motivation, you will need to give them the tools that bring about change via CBT. Whilst doing this, you will also need to try to empower them to use these new skills (this is where the *ready* and *willing* parts come in). To do so, the practitioner will need to use a combination of what is known as 'motivational skills' to avoid the client disengaging. More later on.

Now, before we continue any further, it is important that I explain a critical skill that should be used alongside any form of work undertaken with offenders. It is known as *Pro-Social Modelling*.

Pro-Social Modelling is currently employed as a strategy to tackle offending in its own right, but within the context of this book, I would like you to consider using it alongside the skills that I will describe to empower offenders. But let's define it first!

In my view, Pro-Social Modelling, is best defined by Winstone and Hobbs (2006), who stated it as being:

"A set of specific attitudes and behaviours comprising of a particular style of supervision… the practice of such as offering praise and rewards for pro-social expressions and actions… the probation officer becomes a positive role model acting to reinforce pro-social or non criminogenic behaviour."

Winstone and Hobbs go on to explain that there are four main principles for Pro-Social Modelling. These are:

- Developing a high quality relationship
- Effective modelling
- Effective reinforcement
- Communicating clear targets in attitudes and thinking

To assist further, I will explain what each principle means with regards to working with offenders. Please spend time getting to grips with these principles as, in my view, they are vital for learning how to address offending behaviour and building working relationships.

Developing a high quality relationship

A high quality relationship is defined as a relationship in which the 'give and take' analogy should be used. It is a relationship based on honesty, trust and consistency. A practitioner should not make promises that they cannot keep and the practitioner should always be transparent about their intent.

Demonstrating effective modelling

Copy me! Do as I do! Demonstrate by example! If you want people to act in a specific way, then you should be doing it yourself. I believe this to be core when working with offending behaviour.

For example, if you want someone not to swear then do not swear yourself when talking to them. If something ever slips out, apologise and rather than justifying or denying the behaviour, seek to ensure that it will not happen again. Commit to that promise.

If you do manage to get this form of reciprocal modelling up and running, you will need to ensure that the client feels comfortable when they make mistakes! It is your responsibility to create this safe environment. In order to do this, simply explain that it is okay to make the occasional mistake as long as we learn from it.

Delivering effective reinforcement

Effective reinforcement is all about structure, setting boundaries and expectations for the work to be undertaken, justifiable actions, and following through with what you say is going to happen. For example, before the start of a group session, behavioural boundaries should be set (group rules), clear objectives as to what the session is seeking to accomplish should be presented, and these should be adhered to. If not, prompt action should be taken to challenge inappropriate behaviour.

Displaying clear targets in attitudes and thinking

Communicate with clients. Always give a purpose and direction to sessions with offenders and explain your reasons for actions. This is also known as setting a contract. For example, should you be addressing anger management, explain *why* you will be addressing areas such as belief systems (see chapter on working with violent offenders).

In my experience, practitioners should seek to implement all the principles of Pro-Social Modelling into their daily practice when working with clients. It is important that the practitioner takes responsibility for this and challenges colleagues should they be acting in a manner which is not in line with pro social behaviours and attitudes. However, please *do not* challenge other practitioners openly in front of offenders. Additionally, be cautious of when, where, and how you challenge other professionals who you may work with. If this is done wrongly, it can be very disempowering for that person and they may not even know that they are doing something wrong. Consider talking to that person in private and explaining how uncomfortable you were made to feel and the issue at hand that you wish to address. This is an assertiveness skill (see chapter working with offenders with emotional difficulties).

Once a practitioner has understood the nature of Pro-Social Modelling I believe that it provides the practitioner with a basic structure of how to work with *any offender*.

The Principles of Motivational Work

The principles of motivational work are centred around four core principles.

- Expressing empathy
- Developing discrepancies
- Rolling with resistance
- Supporting self-efficacy

Expressing empathy

Empathy means being able to place yourself in someone else's position and viewpoint, from where you are able to recognise their feelings and understand their thoughts. Being able to do this creates a safe environment in which a client can express their feelings. The practitioner should note that having an understanding of their client's feelings and experiences assists in the process of change. Do not confuse empathy with sympathy. Sympathy is where you actually experience (i.e. share) similar feelings to an individual. As such, judgement can become clouded and sympathy, in my experience, always tends to lead to collusion in one way or another.

Here is an example of how dangerous sympathy can be. On one occasion, I was asked to change a proposal for a Pre-Sentence Report because one of the report's gatekeepers *"liked xx and thought xx was a nice young person who had just been misunderstood and had a hard life."* This was despite a rigorous assessment being undertaken which found *xx* to be dangerous. Needless to say, I did not change the proposal, and was rather shocked by the idea of changing it.

Develop discrepancy

The concept of developing discrepancies sees the practitioner assisting the offender in recognising positive reasons for change. To do this, the practitioner will explore the differences between what the client 'wants' and how they are actually behaving.

When working on the skill of developing discrepancies, you should ensure that you use plenty of open questions, such as "Tell me how your current behaviour is helping you reach your goal." Just remember to keep things simple. One way to remind yourself how this skill works is by remembering this:

Help the client understand the difference between their wants and how they are behaving now.

It is important to point out that developing discrepancies is not just about behaviour. It is also about changing the client's thinking. The existence of discrepancies can be used to address issues such as denial, minimisation and level of substance misuse. It is a useful skill on its own merits during the preparation of a PSR.

Roll with resistance

To me, resistance means the ways in which an offender puts up different obstacles to change. Examples of how someone may be resistant include: ignoring your questions, interrupting you, arguing with you, or denying their behaviour.

We should recognise that when we encounter resistance in an offender it is a sign that we need to change the approach we are using. The practitioner should not take resistance personally.

Overcoming resistance is a bit like a *trial and error* game – the practitioner often has to keep trying different skills until he or she gets it right. When you deploy the right skill, you will immediately see positive results as the client will begin to talk and open up to you. Try it!

In my opinion, you should not challenge resistance directly through the use of negative sayings (e.g. statements such as "No, that is wrong") rather you should explore the offender's behaviour as you did above when developing discrepancies. Assist the client where possible in helping them come to their own solutions while adapting your approach to make this happen. This gives them ownership.

Let's return to how offenders can be resistant. The most common ways I have seen with offenders that plead not guilty at trial is *arguing*. I will therefore broach how I have addressed this in my own practice.

Generally, when an offender expresses a viewpoint, we may sometimes feel as though we need to correct it. This can be very tempting at times and very easy to do. However, if we do this then we often fall into the trap of starting an argument and now the offender has become even more resistant to change. So what should we do? We should be aware that an argument is about to happen!

Use your *reflective listening* skills. Summarise what the other person has said, and seek to explore their opinions. Open up with questions such as "So you said…" or "Having just heard you, you said…" then, follow these statements by asking the client for their viewpoint in a more specific way and whether you have understood what they said correctly. Remember you are exploring their opinions. Here, some useful questions that can be asked include: "What do you think?" or "Can you help me understand *how* or *why*…?"

By exploring the offender's world and opinions, you can get them to come around to your way of thinking through the recognition that their reasoning is unsound.

Remember - you are there to *facilitate* change, not to force it to happen. Also, resistance can often be a way for an offender to get you to explore other parts of their life that have not been covered so far.

Support self-efficacy

As a practitioner, you should value your client as an individual. Your role is to support them and assist where possible with the change process. Clients should be held responsible for choosing and carrying out any actions to change. This will increase their level of self-worth and sustain any changes made in the long term.

The Cycle of Change

Assuming that the practitioner has now equipped themselves with the knowledge of Pro-Social Modelling and the principles of how to undertake motivational work, I will now explain the different levels of motivation. Following this, I will explain the basics of how to undertake motivational interviewing.

In the change process, the client will pass through what is known as the *cycle of change*. Understanding the cycle of change is important in understanding and knowing how to work with any one client at any one time, and thus important in relationship building.

The cycle of change is described by DiClemente and Prochaska (1982, 1983) cited in Fleet and Annison (2003) as a change process which involves moving from a stage of pre-contemplation where offenders are oblivious to any problems, through to contemplation where discontent and ambivalence towards the current state begins, followed by a rapid move through decision to action as the choice to change is made and goals are set. Following this, the client then enters into the Maintenance phase.

Maintenance involves sustaining this change to establish behaviour and ultimately exit the cycle. There is a potential for old behaviours to be revisited and this may result in lapse, where it is either possible to reflect on an incident (moving back around the cycle to maintenance) or to relapse where the decision to change is abandoned and the cycle is exited to a state of contemplation (Winstone and Hobbs, 2006:262-8). Here is a diagram to help the visual learners amongst you.

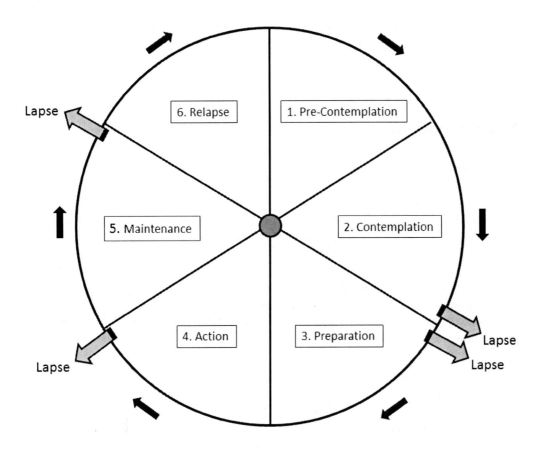

Before we move on, it is worth mentioning that there is some debate as to whether you actually ever exit the cycle of change or if you actually just stay in the maintenance phase (unless you lapse of course). To me though the idea of never exiting the cycle is a little depressing and so I tend to prefer the exiting option. Also, when you explain to the client that you *can* exit the cycle, I like to think that you begin to build on an offender's hope for change.

A client may pass through the cycle of change a number of times. They may also move back and forth between its sections - therefore, it is critical to keep on top of where they are! In my mind, there is absolutely no point in trying to change a client if you *do not know where the client is in the cycle of change*. This idea is explored throughout the book but let me take you back to the principle of 'being specific' in SMART goal setting (discussed in chapter one). How can we set appropriate goals and target the right intervention exercises if we do not approach the offender in the right way? And how can we approach the offender in the right way if we do not know where they are in the cycle of change?

Here, it is worth recognising that explaining the cycle of change to the offender is of equal importance to knowing it yourself. Often, I take a diagram into my sessions to show the offender. Or sometimes I explain the model and draw its sections as I go along - starting with an example that is not based around offending behaviour. Such as stopping smoking.

Motivational interviewing

To move an offender along the stages of the cycle of change, we use the skill of motivational interviewing. This is defined as *"a useful technique to help engage offenders in the process of change."* (Hopkinson and Rex, 2003: 172). And, as you will see, motivational interviewing incorporates all the principles of showing empathy, developing discrepancies, avoiding arguments, rolling with resistance and supporting efficacy (Hopkinson and Rex, 2003) described earlier.

The main aim here is to engage the offender in the cycle of change process (Prochaska and Di Clemente, 1984: 23) and to develop trust and respect. We need to use motivational work in all elements of our work with offenders. This, in brief, is how you carry out motivational interviewing:

- Use affirmation
- Listen to what the client is saying
- Use open questions throughout
- Summarise what is being said
- Find and use self-motivating statements

Using affirmation

Affirmation is praising positive behaviour. Personally, after many years of arguing the opposite in a rather Pavlovian style (!), I have found that affirmation works much better than punishing negative behaviour.

When giving affirmation, the practitioner needs to be very *observant* as sometimes the offender has only made very subtle changes. In addition to this, the practitioner needs to be *specific* with what behaviour they are praising. For example, when working with someone who has abstained from drugs for a week, do not simply say: "You really are doing a great job." Instead, what you should say is: "I notice you have stayed off the drugs for a week now – that is great work."

Listen to what the client is saying; use open questions and summarise

Listen, listen, and listen some more! *Being an expert listener* has the capacity to build up any relationship. By listening well, we also gain the chance to hear more information that could potentially be related to changes in risk levels - 'Say less, hear more...'

This can not only be applied to work, but it can also be used at home (I try to use this every day). Should a client feel that they are not being listened to, or if they feel that they are being misunderstood, it can often lead to a breakdown in the effectiveness of your working relationship.

To be a good listener, you should recognise the various factors involved. These include: knowing the basics of using open questions, reflective listening, and remembering what has been said.

To assist further, I have broken down listening skills into four key elements:

Pay Attention to the information. It is easy to wander off and listen to those voices in the back of your head that may be singing random songs, or whatever else, when someone is talking to you. However, remember why you are doing this role, and that you want to do it to the best of your ability. You will not be able to do it if you do not really understand what is going on.

Reflective listening and feedback. We are naturally affected by our own belief systems which can, in a manner, filter what we hear and what we choose to hear. You should therefore always seek to clarify what has been said with the client, and whether you have misunderstood it in any way. One way to do this when talking to an offender is to use reflective questions such as: "What I am hearing is..." or "It very much sounds to me as though..."

Avoid trying to judge, or interrupting the client. On the point of interrupting, after asking a question, sometimes you may get a very long silence. This is okay. The offender is probably thinking or even waiting for you to break the silence so that they do not have to talk. So do not attempt to jump in straight away unless you really have to, such as telling the client something that is really important. Generally, do not be worried about silence. I have probably in all my years, only spent one whole session in absolute silence, so it is rare - even with a very resistant offender. Often an offender will talk out of boredom or embarrassment. In my mind, it does not matter 'why', as at least they are talking.

Also, if we do not give a client the time to speak, and interrupt them (should they be talking or starting to talk) you are disempowering them and you will end up frustrating them. Give them time to finish. Looking at the cycle of change - you want the client to come to their own solutions. This is important for sustained change.

Try to respond appropriately. The practitioner should want to create an environment in which you can allow the client to discuss what they are thinking and feeling. The practitioner's role is to explore matters and assert pro social opinions that challenge harmful beliefs held by the offender should that be required.

Use self-motivating statements. As we have explored earlier, when a person is changing, they begin to go through a sense of discomfort. Therefore, the skill here is to spot self-motivating statements used by the client to help them move past any obstacles that they put in their way. An example of a self-motivating statement is: "I can change."

Open questions are essential for working with offending behaviour and building an effective working relationship. Typically, practitioners can fall into a trap of asking: "Do you remember what happened?" This is a closed question. The response you will often obtain is: "No. I don't." End of conversation right? Instead, the practitioner should always offer open questions along the lines of "Tell me what happened that night?" as this gives the offender limited space to give a closed response.

If I ever get lost with what questions to ask, I always try to remember my What, When, Who, How, and Why questions surrounding the offence. This also gives me a structure to work from.

In circumstances where a client is being unresponsive to your questions or even if the practitioner has asked a closed question and got unhelpful information, you can benefit from using questions that break down the topic you need information on. So, for example, if you need to get an account of the offence, and the offender has said "I don't know," or "I do not remember," then rework the conversation into parts. Start at any point where the offender can remember (even if it is the day before) and ask them step-by-step what happened after that. Then (and this is very important) use *summarising*. This is when you seek to clarify what has been stated and summarise the important elements of disclosure. This shows that you were listening but - do not worry - it is not a memory test!

Tip: Should an offender be closed with you when talking about their offence then try to get hold of any police documents that outline what happened. Explore this with the offender and ask them how much they agree with what has been written down. Normally, you will get a lot of useful information about the client's viewpoint with this approach.

Using the Cycle of Change

To engage the offender with the cycle of change you must use the skills of motivational interviewing, described earlier, throughout the process. However in addition to this, here are a few very general ideas on how to move the individual though the cycle of change using various exercises and motivational skills:

Pre-Contemplation (stage one)

Signs - The client does not acknowledge that they have a problem. They will often state "I do not have a problem," or "I do not need to change anything." The client may also be happy where they are or they may even think that they *cannot* change.

On occasion, the client may state that "the problem" lies with you, the CJS, or even society. Here, try not to get pulled into conspiracy theories too much (they can sound very interesting) but explore them to the point where you can understand where the client is coming from. You may even be surprised what a client can come up with as a justification for their behaviour.

Your goal - To look at the benefits of change for the offender, to help them consider change, and to move the client to contemplation.

Useful exercise - Facilitate a discussion looking at the positives and negatives of the offender's current behaviour. Try listing these behaviours on a piece of paper. Ensure that you put the headings and lists next to each other so that the client can see and compare. Like this:

Positives	Negatives

Useful motivational skills. In my experience, the most useful motivational skills here are - reflective listening, open questions, reflecting discrepancies and obtaining self-motivation statements.

A non-offending example might be where the client does not think they have a problem with smoking. They may say: "I do not need to give up smoking." An

Example of a useful Motivational Interviewing (MI) strategy - might be to say: "Why do you think society makes such a fuss about people smoking?" (Open Question)

Contemplation (stage two)

Signs - The client is in two minds to change and about what they want. Often clients will state "I know it would be better but...." When reflecting on stage two, you may also be able to pick out potential barriers to change. These can be both practical barriers such as transport to attend sessions or even emotional problems such as depression. Examples of what a client may say here include: "I want to get better but I just cannot get there," or "I am too depressed to handle this."

Your goal - To help empower a desire to change (no matter how small) and move the client to the next stage in the cycle (decision). A sign that this is happening is when the client is in two minds about change.

Useful exercise - Discuss how to overcome obstacles and also look at the long term effects of a particular behaviour with the client. Again, if you are looking at overcoming obstacles remember to try to get the offender to come up with the answers. You should just be asking the questions and not giving advice. Also remember that change involves some form of loss. We need to acknowledge this here and plan for it rather than trying to shy away from the point.

An example of overcoming obstacles such as transport is to ask questions such as "What ways could you get to your sessions?" and "Who could bring you to your sessions if you were stuck?" and then consider all the possibilities.

Useful motivational skills. In my experience, the most useful motivational skills here are - discussing the problem at hand, exploring ambivalence, and reflecting discrepancies between how a client is acting now and what they want.

Non-offending example - The client thinks that smoking may be a problem. They may say: "I think I may need to give up smoking."

Example of a useful MI strategy - You could say: "It sounds as though you can see what the problems are with smoking and do not want to go down that route - what do you think?" (Reflective Question)

Decision (stage three)

Signs - The offender has made a decision to change. Quite simply they will say something along the lines of "Right, I am going to do it." On occasion, you might still get a little bit of ambivalence, but by supporting them through this - you help to build up the therapeutic relationship you want.

Your goal - To facilitate a quick and easy movement into action. Show the offender that they can achieve their goals by breaking them down. Achieving the first step can be very powerful.

Useful exercise - You could discuss short term realistic goals. For example, the first step of gaining your driver's licence might be to pick up the form from the post office. Here, it may even be handy to actually draw or write the steps out to allow the client to 'tick them off' as they go along. Doing so creates a working document for you both.

Useful motivational skills - In my experience, the most useful motivational skills here are - reflecting positive behaviours, and reframing back to the client any negative behaviours they had.

Non offending example - The client feels that they need to give up smoking. They may say: "I need to give up smoking."

Example of a useful MI strategy - You could say: "What steps could take to stop smoking?" (Open Question) or "Sounds like you feel you need to stop smoking?" (Reflective Question)

Action (stage four)

Signs - The client is now preparing to change. When they are ready, the decision to change can become *all consuming*. Often they will present themselves as being highly motivated - stating "I *have* to change," or "I *need* to change."

Your goal - To help the client identify clear steps to change, encourage them to take these steps, and move the client to maintenance.

Useful exercise - I have found the 'steps to a goal' exercises useful here. Often, this exercise is used in the decision stage, but in my experience it acts as a guide to keep a client on track when in the action phase.

The *steps to a goal* exercise basically involves breaking down larger goals into manageable steps. It is important to recognise how 'large goals' are very individualistic. One person's smaller goal is another's large goal.

One quick example of a large goal being broken down into smaller steps expands on the example of trying to obtain a driving licence. Ask the client to break down all the steps they need to take to obtain it. For example:

Step 1. Go to the post office to obtain a provisional licence form

Step 2. Fill the form in and send it off

Step 3. Find out how much lessons are and call around for the best deal

Step 4. Book the lessons and take the theory test

Step 5. Take lessons

Step 6. Take the practical test (large goal achieved if passed)

Useful motivational skills - The most useful motivational skills here are affirmation, lots of reflective listening and using open questions. Also give plenty of feedback on positive behaviour.

Non-offending example - The client has given up smoking. They may say: "I have stopped smoking now" and/or "I am taking an NHS group work programme to help me."

Example of a useful MI strategy - You could say: "You have done really well to stop smoking for one week now. You have also followed the steps you agreed to take at every point. What kind of things could you do to make sure you keep this level of motivation?" (Open and reflective question).

Tip: Should a client struggle with finding goals, you could undertake a simple dreaming exercise. Get them to close their eyes for a minute (if they trust you) and ask them to think about all the things they would like in an ideal world. Give them time to think. This should be for about a minute. However during this time, pose questions such as "How would you like your life to be?", "What would you want in an ideal world?" Then write them all down on paper and start to break down the goals.

Maintenance (stage five)

Signs - Often you will notice at stage five that the offender will make a conscious effort to change but can still have a few ambivalent thoughts racing through their mind.

Be careful here, as your work is far from done. The client can exit the cycle here very easily and fall back briefly to their old behaviour. This is normal and should not be seen as a failure.

Your goal - To encourage the client, monitor them, and identify positive support networks around them. This includes creating a plan of action just in case the offender lapses or relapses. This is formally known as creating a *relapse prevention plan* or a *contingency plan.* Relapse prevention is critical when working with offenders. And it is important to put the plan together when they are motivated.

I am now going to explain how to create a relapse prevention plan, but remember to ensure that when you undertake the exercise – the focus is not towards the negative. It is not about planning for failure. It is about planning for what could go wrong. Life can be very unpredictable. I have found that doing this exercise gives the offender structure and acts as a guide for them to refer to when you are not around. So here it is - simply answer the following questions and write the answers on paper with the offender under the respective headings.

Contingency Plan

- Identify your (the offender's) life history and lifestyle factors that led to the problem (e.g. drugs).
- Identify immediate high risk situations (When you are most likely to undertake the problematic behaviour?).
- Identify what you were thinking, feeling and doing (wrong) when you decided to undertake the problematic behaviour.
- Identify what you will do to cope. (E.g. skills needed, who is your support network, and how could you change your lifestyle?).
- Identify what you will do if you lapse (how will you get back on track as soon as possible).
- Identify how you will maintain your treatment gains and stay away from the problematic behaviour.

Tip: In relation to support networks, ask the client to consider utilising other organisations, as well as family and friends.

Useful motivational skills - In my experience, the most useful motivational skills here are - affirmation, positive feedback, overcoming ambivalence and securing self-motivating statements.

Non offending example - The offender needs motivation to maintain his or her abstinence from smoking.

Example of a useful MI strategy - You could ask: "What kind of thoughts are you going to tell yourself to keep motivated?" (Open Questions)

Lapse and Relapse (stage six)

Signs - Before we explore lapse and relapse, it is important that I highlight the difference between the two, and explain how this stage works in the cycle of change. Lapse and relapse are interlinked in many ways and can be seen as additional stages in the cycle of change.

- Lapse means that a client temporarily returns to their old behaviour. Here they can return back through the cycle to maintenance quickly.
- Relapse means that they have returned back to pre-contemplation or completely exited the cycle.

Your goal - Arguably in both lapse and relapse, your goal is to show the client that it is only temporary, and you should try to move them back to maintenance. For me, the lapse stage is a particularly critical one. It can enable the offender to see the reality of the difficulties they are facing in relation to change. If these are highlighted then it is important to discuss them and ways around them. Also, remember to remind the offender that if they do lapse, this is a normal part of the change process.

Useful motivational skills - The most useful motivational skills here are - showing empathy, using open questions, and exploring ambivalence.

Non-offending example - The offender may or may not smoke again as a one off or completely relapse into smoking as they did before. They may say "I knew I couldn't do it!"

Example of a useful MI strategy - You could say: "I understand that you feel that you need to smoke to relieve stress, but previously you have told me that you did not need it and can do other thing to relieve stress, You have also said that this is a one off - what could you do to stop this from happening again?" (Reflective and Open Questioning)

When considering the cycle of change, it is important for the practitioner and offender to note that the offender can pass through the whole, or parts of the cycle, a number of times per day or even in one session.

A Complicated Relationship (stick with it)

When working with offending behaviour, you may become frustrated by your client's behaviour. At times, you may have negative thoughts / voices in your head telling you that they are testing your patience.

My advice here is to always remain confident in yourself and recognise that the client's behaviour is probably because they are unable to express themselves appropriately or because they are not responding to the particular skill you are using. Additionally, they might not be used to someone helping them and are testing you out - waiting to see if you will actually stick by them.

The best example I can give of this is with Charlie.

Charlie was assessed as having significant anger management issues. He was deemed a challenge by every practitioner he worked with. In a way this was part of the problem. He pushed people away because he did not want to talk about his feelings. He would test workers, forcing them away, as this was what he was used to doing. It was only when a worker I know did not 'give up' on him that he slowly began to trust the practitioner and began to open up and talk about the attitudes and feelings behind his actions. Ironically Charlie is now undertaking a course to become a counsellor.

When working with offenders, an important tip I would offer is to avoid stereotypes and labelling. These impact heavily on the working relationship. In my view, there is nothing more powerful than when someone who sees themselves as a criminal is labelled as such, e.g. a practitioner verbalising "You are in fact a criminal, and bad." This can make the individual feel that they cannot change, and so negative thoughts take over - leading them to re-offend. An example of a negative thought here is "They think I will not change, so what is the point? I may as well carry on."

Labelling can have extremely negative consequences. I have seen some extremely poor practice in my time including practitioners doing exactly the above and labelling people as bad or dangerous *to their face*. I have also worked with offenders who label themselves as bad and beyond help. However, I would like to highlight here that it is not the individual that is bad, only that part of their behaviour which is. In fact, there are very few dangerous people in this world, and in order for us to determine dangerous individuals these offenders pass through further robust assessments that are not explored in this book.

On one occasion, I witnessed an experienced officer tell a client that he was a dangerous alcoholic in front of several other people. Needless to say, and without taking responsibility away from that individual, this had a significant impact on the client's self-esteem and indeed later that day the client violently assaulted someone following a drinking binge. How do I know this? He was later allocated to me.

On a more positive note, I have seen some excellent practice, especially within the realm of modelling behaviour. This is key to a relationship building strategy and can give the client someone to aspire to be like. In fact, some officers are so good at this, I have often thought to myself: "I want to be like that!" and so tried to copy how they do things. So it is important to remember that pro social modelling is not just something we do with an offender; it is a foundation for our own behaviour which can, in effect, be copied by others.

Enhancing the Power of Motivational Interviewing

When attempting to build a relationship with a client, non-verbal communication is just as important as verbal communication. Here is some advice on how to build on those skills and enhance the power of motivational interviewing.

Body language

Understanding body language to its fullest extent is a complicated business and would require a whole other book to explain properly. However, when building a relationship with an offender here are two of the basics you should consider:

Be mindful of your posture. When working with clients, you should have an open posture with appropriate distance between you and the client at all times. The proximity of comfortable distance between the practitioner and client can vary from individual to individual, however I would generally advise that it is the closest distance in which you both feel comfortable.

If you are not sure about where you are sitting or standing, simply ask the client if they feel comfortable with where you are. Sometimes their own body language or actions may clearly indicate that they are not comfortable. A good example is what I call the 'Jeremy Kyle' effect. This is when a guest on the Jeremy Kyle show walks on stage and moves their chair away immediately. From this action alone, you can make several assumptions of their mood.

Eye contact and head nodding. Body language also includes eye contact. My advice here is to avoid staring at your client. This may make them feel intimidated and look as though you are being aggressive. Additionally, it may remind them of situations where they have been in a confrontational situation leading them to subconsciously shut down when talking to you.

While the offender is talking, simple actions (such as a nod of the head every now and again) will give non-verbal signals that you are listening and open to what the offender is saying.

Tip: Okay, so this is not exactly body language but refers instead to tone, volume and tenor of voice. When an offender starts to becomes vocally aggressive, lower your tone and volume, it acts as a direct opposite to what they are doing and the client will have to slow down a little to hear what you are saying. This gives you an opportunity to calm the situation down.

Supercharging the Working Relationship

One way to supercharge the relationship process is to undertake a quick and basic assessment of your client's learning style. This is relevant to any organisation that wants to build a relationship with a client and it is highly important in the learning process. We all learn in different ways, and these can be divided into three core learning styles. These are visual, auditory and kinaesthetic (Fleming's VARK model).

- *Visual* - these are individuals who learn by seeing. Visual learning can be undertaken through many forms such as pictures, visual aids, and diagrams.
- *Auditory* - these are individuals who learn by listening. Learning is best achieved through discussions, conversations and lectures.
- *Kinaesthetic* - individuals who learn by 'carrying out physical activities'. For example, touching and doing things.

Knowing which style your client prefers to learn through is powerful to know but, in my experience, is very much an underused approach within many organisations. For example, within the Probation and Youth Offending Services, the assessment itself seems to be more down to the practitioner's discretion rather than as part of any form of protocol. Imagine trying to teach a kinaesthetic learner in an auditory way! Surely this is one way to disengage a client?

Of course, it is possible for individuals to have a mixture of learning styles depending on the subject area. In turn, people can learn in different ways despite having a preference for a specific learning style. If you have identified a preferred learning style, consider the following ideas for work with offenders:

- *Visual* - consider employing worksheets and even posters especially with young offenders.
- *Auditory* - consider having structured discussions about topics that need addressing.
- *Kinaesthetic* - consider role play and 'skills practice' exercises with individuals.

When undertaking any form of intervention, it is important that if you undertake a group activity that you consider *all the above* learning styles and try to incorporate a mixture of exercises. On a one-to-one basis, and when then client is disengaged with the change process, keep broaching the issue of change from the perspective of their learning style.

Not Just About Working Relationships

While building a healthy working relationship is important, it is not the only factor in reducing recidivism. Reducing offending behaviour or changing behaviour relies on addressing a number of areas including the offence, internal controls (coping strategies) and external controls (environmental factors).

Offending behaviour needs to be addressed in a systematic and evidence based way. Simply trying to build a good relationship is not enough but *it is a critical part* in the process of change.

A word of warning: the practitioner has to ensure that they do not begin to collude with the offender in any way. The practitioner should be challenging the offender as needed.

When working with offenders (and as touched upon above), do not be afraid to say you have made a mistake. Of course, in this type of profession mistakes can have significant consequences, but some mistakes do happen and are normal. Nobody is perfect, and as human beings we are fallible. Simply admit if you are to blame, seek a resolution and never be overly defensive on a point you know to be false or untrue. Offenders will respect you more and will see you as a real person.

Throughout this chapter, I have expressed methods which are currently being used by practitioners today. They have also been very effective in my own practice but, before moving forwards, let's take a moment to consider the false understanding of motivational interviewing and the cycle of change.

Motivational interviewing *does not* mean that the practitioner has to miraculously change into a motivational speaker every time they are in a session with a client. This can in fact be counter-productive. There is nothing worse than motivating someone to do something when they have not got the means to actually do it. However, it is not for you to say that your offender cannot achieve what they want. You have to help them see for themselves whether or not their goal is SMART. So, for example, let's say (on the extreme end) your offender who has no job or qualifications comes in and announces: "I want to be an astronaut."

While we may think that this is not possible - who are we to demotivate them? In this circumstance, I would probably say: "Great, how are you going to achieve this?" and the offender may then begin to break down this huge goal and realise that it is not realistic. Subsequently, they may well change their goal to something else they want - such as gaining qualifications.

Summary

Expressed within this chapter is the idea that the relationship between the client and the practitioner is one of the most important factors in addressing offending behaviour. Additionally, an effective working relationship can be very difficult to achieve. The skills needed to achieve an effective working relationship must be mastered by all those who seek to address offending behaviour.

Learning the skills to engage an offender and elicit change takes time, but by learning them and using them regularly you will soon see the benefits of your efforts with your clients.

In my experience, the principles, concepts and the basic techniques of CBT need to be understood by practitioners. They should also be practiced on a regular basis to ensure we know how to use them effectively. So find time, be creative, and rehearse them!

When it comes to motivational interviewing, the practitioner, generally speaking, should learn to be an expert listener, be proficient in the use of open questions, and be confident in exploring their client's thoughts and feelings. These skills develop over time and by getting a client to open up to you - it is my view that you are naturally building a trusting relationship.

As we saw in the last chapter, and this one, offending behaviour is dynamic. This means that it is always changing and is multi-factorial. A combination of strategies and skills to address it is therefore needed. This, as stressed above, is dependent on what stage of the cycle of change the client is in.

The current evidence in the field supports the idea that the skills and techniques described in this chapter 'work'. So it is important for the practitioner to use them in their practice when needed.

Chapter 2

In the next chapter, we shall be exploring how practitioners address substance misuse in the Criminal Justice System. We shall break things down into two elements which are alcohol misuse and drug misuse. Onwards!

3

Working with Individuals who Offend and Misuse Substances

At the risk of sounding overly morbid, when addressing substance misuse the harsh reality is that practitioners may very well see death, serious injury and significant self-harm issues. It is therefore important that the practitioner knows, at the very least, the basics of how to address substance misuse. In this chapter, I will tell you where to begin!

When considering how to tackle drug and alcohol misuse, one of the big questions a practitioner may ask is: how do you stop or minimise a client's substance abuse when *you* can clearly see that it is so destructive in their life and yet sometimes *they* do not?

In this chapter, we shall explore how I have addressed alcohol and drug misuse within the Probation Service and YOS. We will also examine how drugs and alcohol can interact with each other. To assist in the understanding of this subject area, I will discuss alcohol separately to illegal and legal drugs before combining the topics.

Throughout the chapter, suggestions will be made on how to address substance misuse as a whole and how, from my own understanding, to put CBT and current practice measures in place.

To start this chapter, I will begin with a few reflections to provide context to this topic which will hopefully explain why we are discussing substance misuse in this book.

Note: On occasion, I will refer to legal and illegal drugs as *substances* given the sheer number of different forms available. Additionally, I will also refer to the term *substance misuse* from a more general perspective and with reference to alcohol also. But do not worry - what I am referring to will be made clear at the time.

A Moment of Reflection on Substance Misuse

Although many probation offices have changed in recent times, I recall the first time I stepped into a probation office interview room as a trainee. The smell was similar to what you might expect in a popular public house on a Sunday morning after a busy Saturday night. I will never forget that stagnant smell. I am now, however, rather accustomed to it.

As a trainee, I had little appreciation for the complexities of alcoholism or substance misuse as a whole. I always felt that the Probation Service had the answers and that there must be some *magic cure* that I was simply waiting to learn.

In reality, this was a rather fantastical view: substance misuse is far more complex than this. In fact, it is one of the most difficult areas to address with any offender. Why? At the end of the day, when all the chips are down, it relies on that individual person to make the decision to change and maintain those changes.

The process of change is often not helped by the environment the client may have to return to during any period of abstinence. For example, a client may abstain from alcohol use whilst in custody, present themselves as *motivated* to remain that way on release, and then (on the first day of release) temptation will prove too much and the client relapses. In addition, these individuals are frequently not helped by their respective circles of peers who will often encourage them to drink.

Alcohol: In my experience, alcohol is one of the most dangerous and readily available drugs today. It underpins, as a *disinhibitor,* many offences and is often used as an excuse or a client's 'reason' for anti-social behaviour. For example, a client will often tell me: "It was the drink, not me!"

In reality, I feel that, as a community, we need to move people away from the preconception that alcohol causes behaviour. This takes away our ownership of the problem at hand and makes an assumption that if we stop using alcohol all our problems will just disappear.

In very simplistic terms, alcohol *does not* cause an individual to behave in a specific way. Alcohol simply makes it easier for the client to make a decision. What alcohol can do is distort the reality of the situation.

In my experience, alcohol misuse is hard to change. Sometimes even more so than drugs. Alcohol is often glamorised by the media as a coping mechanism for difficult problems.

Look at television. How often have you seen a character tell another something to the effect of "Let's go get a drink and you can tell me all about it," or a character taking solace in a bottle of Scotch when life plays them a bad hand? Surely this has some impact on people?

Now, I do not intend for the reader to assume that I am against drinking alcohol. I drink alcohol myself, and in moderation it's fine. I am merely stating that the full effects and significance of alcohol misuse are misunderstood, and not addressed correctly within schools and society as a whole. In turn, alcohol also has significant cost implications upon society. For example, imagine the cost involved in dealing with an individual who has been in a drunken brawl and arrested? Purely from a procedural standpoint, think about the cost of police time, the court's time, Probation / YOS time, and solicitor time. Then imagine where else this money could go? Especially with regards to the National Health Service (NHS) if they were involved.

Some Points on Addressing Substance Misuse as a Whole

Before we start, I would like to share a tip, and a word of caution which was touched upon in chapter two. This was also first shared with me by my first (and my most inspirational) mentor.

Tip: Always start working with a client firmly on the basis of *where they are* in the cycle of change.

Caution: Never assume you know *everything* about a specific topic. Practitioners are always learning from every client they work with. With substance misuse in particular, seek professional support from a specialist worker in this field when needed.

On the cautionary point above, it is important for the practitioner (or agency) to be able to distinguish between a client with whom they *can* provide interventions for, and a client who requires specialist intervention from another professional organisation.

Whilst the Probation Service and YOS are able to make *assessments* of those who have low and high needs, individuals who are assessed as being within the *dependant range* (i.e. high needs) should ideally work with someone with both the relevant experience and qualification(s). This qualification is usually called a DANOS (Drugs and Alcohol National Occupational Standards).

It needs to be pointed out, however, that neither the DANOS qualification (nor any other) is officially needed to work with someone who has substance abuse problems. Anybody can theoretically work quite legally with individuals who have substance issues. This, in my view, illustrates why offenders who enter the Criminal Justice System, or people with substance misuse problems, tend to have varying degrees of satisfaction from services.

When working with individuals who misuse substances, a general rule of thumb is that it is important to work alongside the client's General Practitioner (GP). The GP may have access to a number of resources your organisation does not or which are difficult to reach. In addition, the client may require specific medication to work alongside any form of therapy. It is my standpoint therefore that any practitioner's *first point of call* is to make a referral to a client's GP. If the client is not registered, assist them in doing so. If needs be *do it there and then* if you can.

Recognising Some of the Addictive Characteristics of Drugs and Alcohol

In order to address the problem of substance misuse (both alcohol and drugs) we need to be able to recognise the signs that there is a problem. In my experience, there tend to be many recurring signs of addictive behaviour. These signs can be startlingly obvious, but it is important that practitioners remain aware of them and how individuals can mask these signs in order to hide the problem. Here is a rather comical example of how someone did it in my own practice:

> I recall one offender I worked with as a trainee. She sat in front of me with a bottle of water, sipping it throughout the session, as we discussed how she could make changes to her life.
>
> She was wearing strong perfume which filled the room and this seemed rather a nice change in my mind from the usual smells. The session appeared to go well, however I did notice that she got progressively more tired and lethargic as the session went on.
>
> We managed to achieve the main aims of the session, so we wrapped things up and she left. A short while later I received a call from the receptionist. "Jonathan," she said, "did you notice anything different about your client?" "Not really," I replied. "Although she was a bit lethargic."
>
> The receptionist then explained that when she went to clear the room out, she found the bottle of water, and it was in fact filled with pure vodka. My client had sat with me, getting progressively more and more drunk, during our session.

Yes, I perhaps should have picked up on this sooner, but the purpose of this anecdote is to draw your attention to the lengths some people resort to in hiding their problems. Then again, the critical reader may assume that she left the bottle to 'subtly tell me the problem'!

Despite the above, I would like to outline some of the more common characteristics of addictive behaviour:

- The first and probably most common sign for both alcohol and drugs, which can be difficult to hide, is a clear *pre-occupation* with *use* or even the idea of *non-use*. An example here is when a client clearly states how they will often consume or use alcohol or drugs on a daily basis to deal with problems or just to "get by". Or the client attends a session intoxicated and the *whole* meeting is dominated by the discussion of abstinence.
- The client will *use alone* (i.e. by themselves) and is content with doing this. When considering alcohol users, this is why it's a common assessment question with alcohol assessments to ask: "Do you drink alone or with others?" Often there is a mixture of the two; if the client is perfectly "happy" drinking alcohol alone – this can be a sign of addictive behaviour.
- A client may use alcohol or drugs as a form of self-medication to help them relax or even get stimulated. For example, I have heard the argument many times from offenders that they use cannabis for 'medicinal purposes'.

   When considering alcohol, we have to remember that this is a complex drug and can give either feelings of *highs* or *lows*. Here a client will state something within the realms of "I need it to relax," or "I need it to get up in the morning."

- The client will continue to use alcohol or drugs despite the damaging consequences it brings to that individual. This position also includes the idea that the client continues to misuse substances despite continued expressed concerns by a professional, family or friends.
- The client will have a higher tolerance or capacity than the norm. Here you may often hear a client say: "I can drink ten pints and it does not really affect me!" or "A little bit of cannabis will not hurt anyone!"
- Protection of supply. Here a client will be overly protective of their supply. If they do not have it, they can spend a significant amount of time seeking it which can lead to offending behaviour. For example, stealing to sell goods to obtain money to purchase drugs or alcohol.

These are only a few of the characteristics of addiction. There are more physical and psychological symptoms. However these are ones I have seen very commonly with my clients.

With regards to what to look out for, and as mentioned earlier, some of the signs of addictive behaviour may appear obvious, but it is down to the professional to spot them.

This can be very hard if the offender is trying to mask it. In turn, whilst the signs may be very clear to you, discussion with the client may reveal that they do not recognise their behaviour as a sign of dependency or a problem.

Working with Alcohol Misuse

Having broached the characteristics of substance misuse, let us now turn our attention to focus on two of the different typologies of alcohol users (very common within the Probation Service) and then look to how we can begin to address alcohol abuse.

Binge drinkers

Binge drinkers will *often* state that they "drink to get drunk". They will consume large amounts of alcohol in a short period of time. In my experience the numbers of offenders who fall within this bracket tend to be under 25 years old, and are more likely to be men than women. However I feel that this is starting to balance out within the general population.

From an offending point of view, I have also found that men, in general, tend to be at a higher risk of being a victim or committing violent offences while under the influence of alcohol.

Chronic drinkers

Chronic drinkers are also known as dependant drinkers and tend to be over the age of 30 years old and once again are more likely to be men (especially within the Criminal Justice System).

Chronic drinkers consume large amounts of alcohol on a regular basis and are at significant risk from a variety of health problems including strokes and cancer.

The Starting Point of Addressing Alcohol

Currently I feel that the Probation Service and YOS are beginning to 'get it right' when addressing alcohol misuse. This is through the guidance of work developed by the World Health Organisation (WHO) called *brief intervention*.

Brief intervention is a straightforward but highly effective tool that is an 'assessment and personalised discussion' of a client's alcohol consumption level, and how it relates to the general population. It can range from five minutes to several sessions depending on the need and provides advice on reducing consumption in a persuasive but non-judgemental way. It also follows the principles of the cycle of change discussed in chapter two.

It is my belief that any organisation which employs professionals who have an awareness of motivational interviewing (MI), and basic training in delivering brief interventions, has the ability to address alcohol abuse

The principles of Brief Intervention (alcohol)

Brief intervention is fundamentally about getting accurate information on an individual's alcohol misuse, getting the client to 'think' about the misuse, and assisting them in minimising the risks associated with alcohol. This includes not only risks to the client but also, in the context of this book, harm to others and a reduction in reoffending.

Tip: Remember that when professionals undertake brief interventions, they are attempting to minimise, not remove, alcohol use in the safest possible way.

In order to undertake brief interventions, the practitioner should recognise the following principles:

1. You should start by undertaking an assessment of the problem. This can be through a simple questionnaire which is called an alcohol audit.
2. Continuously, as a practitioner, be non-judgemental and place an emphasis on personal choice and personal responsibility. You are giving the client ownership of the problem; change will be their decision not yours.
3. Give non-judgemental advice on how the client could change their behaviour and offer them a number of different options. This includes assisting them in *how* to achieve these options through goal setting exercises (as discussed in chapter two).
4. Critically, be empathetic not sympathetic. Try to recognise the problem from the client's standpoint.

Undertaking the Assessment for Brief Intervention

In many situations, you may be faced with a client who does not want to change or does not recognise that they have a problem. How do you tackle this?

Firstly, as explained above, adopt a non-judgmental position, try to put yourself in their shoes, and see things the way the client sees them. Then help the client see how their current behaviour is not conducive to achieving their long term goals. This is achieved through motivational interviewing.

Warning - do not be overly sympathetic with an offender's situation as this may lead to collusion.

Next up is to put a brief intervention in place. I have broken this down into 10 steps with regards to how I undertake the process. Note that I believe this brief intervention should always be undertaken on a one-to-one basis. Why? Because of the personal/private nature of this type of work, and the fact that an individual's reasons for misuse (and strategies for managing misuse), may be completely different from another person's. A brief intervention in a group setting is of dubious value.

The 10 Steps to Doing a Successful Brief Assessment and Intervention

Step 1. Explain to the client that you would like to do a brief assessment with them to look at their drinking patterns. Explain that this is a short process that requires them to be as honest as possible. State that 'should they not tell you the truth', then in reality they are only cheating themselves as it's likely to lead them to a treatment that will not work for them.

This in my experience sets the scene or contract for the session. It also promotes honesty and openness which is important for the working relationship described in the previous chapter.

Step 2. With the client, you then complete a questionnaire known as an alcohol audit questionnaire. This questionnaire asks a series of questions and offers the client a series of possible answers (multiple choice). Each answer generates a static score.

Often the client will automatically guess that the higher the score the more problematic their use is - and so they will be tempted to hide the truth. I therefore tell the client before we start: "Do not worry about the score here, just answer everything as honestly as possible!"

By doing this you are, at the very least, making an attempt to look after the quality and validity of the data obtained.

Step 3. If the client is able, ask *them* to add the final scores together. If they cannot do this, help them but work through it together. One way to do this is to simply ask questions such as "four plus two equals six, right?" or something to that effect.

Step 4. Once you have generated a total score, put a circle around it and tell the client: "Right, this is your score, and this is personal to you."

In order to set some context for discussing scores, let's look at the score ranges for the alcohol audit questionnaire I use. The actual values are not important here (and the scoring system/range will vary between different questionnaires), it is the relative spectrum of drinking misuse, and where people fall, that should be noted:

- If the client scores between 0-7, then they are either Low Risk Drinkers or non-drinkers. Within this area, they will probably not need any intervention. These individuals usually consume alcohol to a limited degree or not at all and their use is not seen as problematic.

- If they score between 8-14, then they will fall within the area of Hazardous Drinkers. This is usually associated with binge drinkers, described earlier. An example here would be the stereotypical image of a university student drinker.

- If the client scores between 15-21, they fall within the area of Harmful Drinkers. Here alcohol users usually have some form of problematic pattern of drinking that will be damaging to them. An example here is an individual who begins to drink on an almost daily basis to excess and fails to recognise the harm being caused to their health and life. However, in contrast, it is becoming even more frequent to find that some individuals who fall in this bracket can function to a high level in extremely difficult roles (such as lawyers, doctors) and no one other than those close to them will recognise that a problem is developing.

- If an individual scores between 22-30 they fall within the Moderately Dependant Drinkers category. Such a score is a significant warning sign to the practitioner; a referral to a specialist agency should be made immediately. Those who fall within this bracket have often developed or are developing significant health problems. Their lifestyle may also be relatively problematic resulting in regular offending behaviour (looking at those within the Criminal Justice System that is).

- And finally, 31-40 indicates Severely Dependant Drinkers. Those who fall within this bracket will most likely have significant health problems already, and they may see alcohol as the main focal point of their life. Individuals here will often seek whatever possible opportunity to obtain and consume alcohol on a daily basis.

Step 5. Before you explain to the client what the score means - reiterate the purpose of the questionnaire and where it comes from. I will often tell the client "You have generated this score. This questionnaire is used by professionals in this field to give an assessment of how your drinking levels compare to disclosed use within the population of the UK. It also will also give us an idea of what treatment route will be most suitable."

Step 6. Now explain that a score of 8 or above (or whatever the threshold score of the questionnaire you use) usually indicates that the client will need to address their alcohol use in some way. You will also need to ensure that you do not allow the client to see the threshold score, as it is usually written somewhere on the questionnaire. This is because on occasion the client may feel that if they are at the 'lower end' of the scoring system then they do not have as big a problem as their representative category suggests.

Step 7. Discuss how the client feels about this for a short period of time. It will usually shock a majority of people, but take time to explain that this score does not define them as a person, nor is it a label. Also, keep away from the phrase "alcoholic". Labelling a person is very powerful if they take on this identity. For example, I recall one client who would often tell me: "Well my doctor said I was an alcoholic, so I am an alcoholic, and there is nothing I can do about it." Ask yourself - how is this conducive to positive change?

Tip: It is worth recognising that the removal of labelling in this system of brief interventions is in stark contrast to that of Alcoholics Anonymous (AA). With AA it is the use of a label (in part) that is employed in order to clearly identify the problem at hand.

Step 8. Now reflect on the score and how it compares to the rest of the population. Some of the more critical clients may ask further questions in relation to the validity of the questionnaire. It is important here that you highlight how the questionnaire is just a method used to give an idea of use and possible treatments.

Step 9. Returning to what was started in step 7, continue the discussion with regards to how the individual feels about the results. It is important to have a definition to hand of what each category means. This can be obtained from the World Health Organisation website.

Step 10. Finally, give some basic advice on safeguarding the user. This should include discussing the consequences of continued use to them, and society around them. Look at possible treatment options and try to motivate the user to engage.

It is not within the remit of this book to give a comprehensive account of how to undertake this intervention or how to address alcohol abuse as a whole. The above outline is simply to prompt ideas, give you a starting point, and to present a few useful exercises. Generally, should a practitioner seek to address alcohol abuse, I believe that the practitioner should obtain as much training as possible. In turn, the methodologies by which the practitioner will complete assessments may change in time as new research is developed.

When reflecting on the categories of alcohol abuse and allocation of resources, I feel that services such as the Probation Service and YOS should concentrate on those who fall in the hazardous and harmful drinker types. Those who fall within moderately dependant and severely dependant categories should be treated by a specialist agency. Scoring within these types should always initiate a referral to such services. However, when I refer to a 'formal referral' this does not mean that you cannot continue with an intervention in the short term. Brief intervention, done correctly, will motivate that individual to undertake treatment.

Some Useful Tips:

Tip 1: When discussing the impact of falling into a specific drinking type, you may wish to try using a cost/benefit analysis, which is described in chapter four. This attempts to motivate the user to reflect on the pros and cons of continued drinking in their present manner.

With regards to reflection, your aim is to move your client from pre-contemplation to contemplation, or if they are in contemplation to decision and action (cycle of change).

Tip 2: You should always, where possible, seek to explore *how* to achieve any goals generated during the session.

Tip 3: It may be a good idea to be as creative as you can with this intervention. Look at your client's learning style(s) and incorporate them into the session. This could include the use of videos, visual aids, role play, or even just discussions. The great thing about brief interventions is that, as long as you stick to the principles, you can be as creative as you like with their implementation.

Probation and YOS Programmes that Address Alcohol Misuse

In chapter one, we looked at the assessments that the Probation Service and YOS use. From these assessments, a practitioner will guide the courts as to what he or she feels are the most suitable sentencing and rehabilitation options, in accordance to strict guidelines that must be followed. These proposals will usually include a comprehensive plan of what work the offender will need to complete to reduce their respective risk level.

The assessment itself often occurs before sentencing and is used as a guide by magistrates or judges. Ultimately, the magistrate or judge could go against any recommendation made by the Probation Service or YOS but generally these services tend to work well together.

With regards to alcohol misuse, a practitioner should always seek to establish, as early as possible, what work is needed to fit any particular offender or client - giving them as great a chance as possible, time-wise, for an effective intervention to take place.

Time is an important factor here. Magistrates or judges will seek guidance from professionals as to how long it is felt the offender will need to complete their rehabilitation. For example, an offender who simply requires advice and guidance on safe drinking may only require work over a three month period to reduce the risks. On the other hand, a dependant drinker may require a period of around two years. These time frames are only examples and judging time frames should be made in accordance with the local availability of resources. For example, if there is a waiting list for a client to go to residential rehabilitation, you will be required to find out how long this waiting list is, and inform the courts accordingly.

In addition, rehabilitation programmes vary from area to area throughout the country depending on what organisation 'has purchased what'. For example, if an area had a particular issue with alcohol related *violence* then a programme would be put in place that specifically addressed this.

Looking at the assessment of alcohol misuse prior to sentence, the practitioner can make a number of recommendations to the court. These range from structured programmes (either on a one-to-one basis or within a group) or an intervention defined as a *specified activity*. This intervention, as discussed in chapter one, is when the client is required to address a specific need for a specific period of time on a specific topic. A good example here is when an offender is assessed as having a problem around becoming aggressive when they are intoxicated. At the time of writing, Thames Valley Probation Service are providing a specified activity named Manage Alcohol Related Aggression (MARA) which lasts 10 sessions, and which is designed to assist in helping clients avoid, cope and escape alcohol fuelled confrontational situations as well as helping individuals control or abstain from alcohol use.

Programmes and Specified Activities

Looking at the differences between programmes and specified activities, there would not seem to be much difference. However, in my view, there are significant differences (based on the fact that I used to quality assure them in previous roles).

Programmes that address alcohol misuse are usually accredited. This means that they have been rigorously tested and proven to show some form of recidivism on offending behaviour. Specified activities are not accredited.

Programmes require a significant amount of oversight to remain accredited and are often expensive to any organisation that uses them. This is because an organisation will need to not only purchase the programme, but retain it, obtain specific training, continuously staff the programme and monitor the delivery of the requirements. Specified activities do not need this and it is down to the discretion of management on the level of oversight that is undertaken.

Now what appears to be happening (most likely due to the economic climate of these services) is that there has been a shift in interventions where accredited programmes are being pushed aside for the cheaper alternative specified activities. The truth of the matter is that anyone theoretically can develop a specified activity. As long as an organisation likes it - they could use it. The effectiveness of these interventions and possible future implications are sometimes questionable however.

The Use of CBT in Alcoholism

Cognitive Behavioural Therapy, in relation to alcohol misuse, is a promoted/endorsed strategy within the Probation Service and YOS. I would therefore like to share a story of how it has worked well on a one-to-one basis, within my own practice, by looking at the case study of Carly.

Carly's parents always had alcohol in the house, and she was given brandy in her milk as a baby to get her to sleep. At the age of 7, her family would regularly give her wine at dinners.

Fast forwarding to the present, Carly did not realise that she had a problem - despite drinking to excess on a regular basis and this being linked to her offending behaviour. It was not until she was diagnosed with diabetes and attended several meetings with myself and other professionals that she thought her drinking might actually be a problem and that she should probably stop. Following a complex route, Carly got a place on a residential detoxification programme. This was a place where she would live without alcohol and address her problem.

After leaving the programme, however, and no matter how hard she tried to stay abstinent, she would start drinking again.

In sessions, we began to work on Carly recording the thoughts and feelings she experienced throughout the day and evening. By analysing the thoughts and feelings Carly had around her alcohol use, she came to understand that she was unable to stick to her goal of quitting drinking, because of her *all-or-nothing* or *black and white* thinking. This, in itself, is known as a negative automatic thought and will be discussed later in this book.

Carly realised that she needed to become abstinent, so every time she had a "slip" she considered herself to have failed, and would drink even more that night, pledging to quit again the next day.

I then explored with her the idea that all-or-nothing thinking was actually sabotaging her attempts to quit. Discussions also uncovered a lot of shame that Carly was experiencing in reaction to her illness, which had compelled her to keep her diabetes secret from her friends and family. And having drunk alcohol for as long as she could remember she simply did not know how to say no to drink.

It was clear. Carly was at the contemplation stage of change so was not ready for complete abstinence (even though her doctor recommended that she should). In recognition of this, we changed her treatment to the goal of controlled drinking. This included a plan of no more than one drink per night, three nights a week.

After having a drink at a social gathering, Carly would leave immediately, and she would not socialise the following night in order to keep on track. In the meantime, she worked on telling friends and family about her health problem, and asked for their support in quitting drinking.

With a more realistic treatment goal, and the support of a few close friends, Carly was able to meet her treatment goal within a month, and within three months, she was finally able to achieve abstinence.

A practitioner, in my view, should have a firm grip and good understanding of CBT before they start to work with offenders. This does not mean a practitioner needs to be a cognitive behavioural therapist. I am merely suggesting that they should have a basic comprehension of CBT, and know the area they are addressing with an offender well. For example, if they are delivering a programme on alcohol related violence they should know this topic appropriately before they try to teach others.

As a practitioner in this field, it is important to be able to *signpost*. If you, as a practitioner, cannot address a specific topic then you need to signpost that client to a place where they *can* get the help they need. Do not pretend to have all the answers.

The Link between Offending and Alcohol

In my experience, alcohol is significantly related to offending behaviour. As a practitioner, if you tackle alcohol misuse, indirectly you will tackle offending. On the front line, it is important to help the offender see this link. However do not simply tell them, explore how their actions can lead to negative outcomes. Also, allow them to recognise that they have a problem with alcohol themselves. Doing this can be very powerful in reducing reoffending.

The above can be achieved through brief interventions, but I shall reiterate how important it is to know your limits as a practitioner. If the client's needs are greater than your individual skillset and knowledge, signpost them to an intervention that can actually help. This could be through programmes or other professional organisations. When you have done this - have a good understanding of what the intervention involves and assist the client on the learning points of the programme or intervention when it finishes. You may also be required to continuously motivate the client to engage in this process throughout its implementation.

Working with Illegal and Legal Drug Misuse

Working with drug misuse on the face of it can seem complicated. But over the years, I have found that probably the most complicated area is how 'working with users' can impact on the practitioner - emotionally.

Looking back over my past experiences, it would seem that no aspect of academia can prepare you for actually working with users. In some ways you must just experience it and learn to cope through implementing the skills of CBT yourself. However, I would like to offer you, the reader, some idea of what you may expect to come across.

In the past, I have worked with some superb practitioners. They have saved clients' lives but never get any recognition other than perhaps an email or two that flies around their respective offices. I have seen many colleagues act in amazing ways where only through quick thinking and staying calm under pressure were practitioners able to save them.

In the most extreme cases, a practitioner working in this field will need to deal with death. I will discuss death in more detail later in this book, but would like to share a story with you now. A story of how death can impact on you as a practitioner.

Let me introduce to you a female client I saw on one occasion for one of my colleagues, when my colleague was ill.

> This client was called Pat. Pat was dependent on heroin and crack cocaine. She would regularly offend via theft to facilitate her habit. She was around 30 years old, but her heavy drug use had clearly had a significant impact on her physically, and she looked much older. I sat in the room with her and noticed how she twitched, continuously licked her lips, and had slight foaming on the side of her mouth. We spoke about her use and she appeared open and honest.
>
> I felt like I had made a huge difference in relation to getting her to finally engage in a specialist service which I know my colleague had been trying for some time. The session went so well that I was in some ways 'buzzing' that I had managed to make a difference.
>
> Two days later, my colleague told me that Pat had overdosed and died. I recall my reaction and simply said: "Oh, are you okay mate?" to which she replied "Yes, just a bit sad." I then went about my routine as normal and did not think about Pat for the rest of my working day.
>
> I drove home and parked the car. As I took the keys out of the ignition I suddenly burst into tears thinking about what I could, or should, have done to help Pat more. Should I have walked her to the clinic to get help? Should I have done something else? Could I have done more?

The truth, in reality, is that as a practitioner you can only do what you can. Your role is to motivate, promote change, support change and, if possible, 'teach the tools' people need to make changes. Try not to take too much ownership of your clients' problems as you will become either overly stressed or (in some cases) highly depressed. These roles are notorious for that.

The Tier System

When addressing substance misuse, there is some excellent guidance on what practitioners (and agencies) should be trying to achieve with their clients. This is based on what is called the *tier system*.

The tier system is quite simply a system by which you can match the type of user with the type of intervention required. It also gives reference to what competencies are recommended for practitioners, and examples of where you might find somebody using the strategies it suggests.

My advice? Stick to it! Discipline yourself and be regimented in your belief about what you can actually achieve, and with whom. As long as you have covered what can be seen as 'best practice' - how can you then be hard on yourself? With this knowledge, feel assured that you are doing all you can within your professional capacity.

The tier system can be split into four main… ahem… tiers.

Tier 1

This is primarily for agencies that require minimal specialist skills to undertake any interventions needed. This can include agencies such as healthcare services, homelessness services, police officers, or Probation and Youth Offending Services. Your role here? To give brief advice to the client, and possibly make a referral to a specialist agency.

How do you tell whether a client falls within this bracket? In essence this would be anyone who you would *not* assess as falling within a 'dependant area' but more specifically those who are identified as presenting use which may be hazardous or harmful. Do you need any qualifications for tier 1 work? Although it is advised that you undertake a DANOS qualification, in reality (and as already mentioned) you do not officially need anything. If you are looking for employment in this field, a lack of DANOS may prove a hindrance, though.

Tier 2

Tier 2 is for agencies that purposely target problematic areas. The services would offer specific advice, on specific areas of need, such as crack cocaine use. At this stage the primary function would be to provide the client with access and support with regards to misuse, as well as assessment and referral to specialist agencies. Those who undertake these roles may work within areas such as hospital accident and emergency departments, Probation Services and Youth Offending Services. These individuals will all be purposefully trying to address those who misuse substances. Your role, on a one-to-one basis, is to make the relevant assessment of use, provide general interventions, and make any required referral.

Tier 3

Tier 3 provides provisional community-based-care planned treatment. This is for clients with more complex needs. They may require support from different agencies (multi-agency working). An example could be the Probation Service or YOS developing a care plan with a local drug agency to address many different problematic areas such as a client with alcohol *and* drug problems. The Probation Service could address the alcohol issue and a different local agency addresses the drug issues.

Tier 4

This is a provision that provides residential (inpatient) care and planned treatment. This is generally for those who fall within the dependant region of assessment and require intensive support. Here the client is, in some ways, isolated from the community and undertakes probably the most difficult period(s) of their life through detoxification.

As a practitioner or budding practitioner, it is important to recognise what tier your organisation and client falls within. Then reflect on what support you can actually offer. As a rule of thumb with substance misuse, if you are concerned about someone's substance misuse whether it be alcohol or drugs:

Make a referral to a General Practitioner, or if you are aware of a local professional agency that addresses the issue – contact them.

When addressing substance misuse, always become familiar with what agencies or services are available to you. Also, seek as much training as possible whether that is in-house or external. You never stop learning and substance misuse especially is an evolving topic; new research introduces new treatment styles and methods as well as fresh information about old and new drugs.

Addressing Substance Misuse in Adults and Youths

When addressing substance misuse between adults and youths, there are some differences, but the general ethos remains the same. I will therefore combine the strategies used to tackle this issue, but also separate advice between adults and youths where needed. As a general rule, I feel that it is important to have some form of context with regards to the interventions you are planning as this will help increase the effectiveness of any intervention you deliver.

Historically, increasing numbers of young people began to use drugs in the 1990s, and since then there have been various government strategies to try and address the problem. This has included 'zero tolerance' approaches to drugs which are in contrast to the idea of 'offender desistance' which revolves around the idea of building a working relationship with individuals and slowly moving them away from offending behaviour and even substance abuse.

There has also been a significant amount of research on the different programmes that have been developed, programmes which vary from structured accredited interventions to one-to-one tailor-made work created by the practitioner. Structured accredited programmes could include programmes such as the Offender Substance Abuse Programme (OSAP). Structured pieces of work can merely mean a well thought-out organised session based on worksheets and discussion.

Focusing on young people specifically, there does appear to be significant evidence to suggest that the effectiveness of current interventions (in relation to substance misuse) within the UK is limited, and has varying degrees of success. I will now discuss why!

Overall it is thought that interventions for young people, at best, offer only a very modest or only short term reduction in the number of people who use drugs. In addition, current young person interventions tend to have even more limited (or no impact) on people who *experiment socially* with different drugs. It seems that if people want to use drugs, they are going to find a way!

Currently in the UK, practitioners have been using what are known as *educational programmes* to address substance misuse. These are based on interventions that seek to deter the young person or adult from substance misuse by highlighting the negative effects of the substance, looking at the dangers of drug use, and teaching social skills such as 'how to say no'.

Why do we use an educational approach if it does not have a significant impact? The answer is that it appears to be one of the few approaches that incorporates CBT. And CBT has statistical backing which is recognised by the government.

When looking at statistical backing for these interventions, problems become apparent (especially in relation to substance misuse). Controlling the different variables underpinning substance misuse can be painstakingly difficult and results will almost always come across as subjective with the potential for bias. This is why many evaluations tend to be inconclusive as a whole. It is my view, therefore, that when you come across new studies - always remain open to them - but critically question them with regards to any knowledge you have previously obtained. This also makes for great discussion amongst your peers.

Studies have suggested in general that programmes which provide the following interventions can offer positive results:

- Those that offer improvement in the knowledge of the subject

- Those that offer ways to make informed decisions

- Those that improve an individual's self-esteem

When undertaking any intervention you should incorporate the above elements.

It is here that I would also like to stress that, when working with young people or even adults, the practitioner should always seek to support the individual to make *choices*. Informed choices at that.

We live in a society and world that provides consequences for our actions. We can, however, change our actions through making better choices. You decide to make a bad choice? Chances are - there will be bad consequences. On the flip side, should you make a good decision - the rewards will come even if they come a little later than expected. By reinforcing this idea, and helping the client make good decisions, you will increase self-esteem and individuality.

To address substance misuse, you must understand the issues that interventions generally have. These will be described as you read on. You will then be able to work around or address the issues that arise. This is what you call being *responsive* to individual needs, and this is one way to increase the effectiveness of any intervention for a client.

Intervention Issues for Alcohol and Drug Users

There is research to show (perhaps surprisingly) that shock/scare tactics surrounding substance misuse in young people is rarely effective in influencing behaviour. In some cases, especially with hardened drug users or dependent drug users, it may in fact increase their excitement and motivation to use those drugs. For example, showing young people pictures of the 'equipment' drug users use may inadvertently educate them and encourage them to use drugs.

The educational interventions described above have other pitfalls. Firstly, in my experience, regular drug users are fully aware of the dangers of use but will still continue to use drugs because 'they like them'. Often, they will formulate a distorted cost/benefit analysis (as described in chapter four) which promotes the short term gains of that specific drug. Often they will fail to recognise or place value on the long term consequences which they may tell themselves 'will never happen" or which are too far away for them to actually care. And as mentioned earlier in the chapter, often the young person may say that "I do it because I like it," or "I do it because I enjoy it."

On this "I do it because I like it" example, I feel that the educational intervention has its benefits. Statements such as this should be a sign to the practitioner as to what they need to do with that client. Here, I would suggest that the practitioner needs to work on the young person's knowledge base and the serious implications of their behaviour, for example, to their own health, to their relationships, and even to the community around them.

In my experience, there is also a common assumption by professionals that young people are pressured by their peers into using drugs. However, this is not always the case. It is often down to an individual's own decision making processes rather than pressure per se. We must therefore help the client to make good decisions. To do this I suggest teaching them the following *problem solving* method (with working example):

1. *Be clear and state what the problem actually is. Be specific!*

Let us suppose a client comes in late to see his officer. He/she then complains that the officer will not see them. They become angry and upset. They protest that their respective officer is not helping them. What is the problem here?

Here, when you get to the core of it, the client is upset that they will be sent a warning letter and may be returned to court. The real problem therefore is that they feel they may be returned to court.

2. *Think of as many different ways (positive and negative) of solving the problem as possible!*

The client should reflect on as many ways as possible they could react both positively and negatively to manage the situation. Getting angry is of course one way, shouting is another, but there are also a number of alternatives such as calling their officer later that day, booking another appointment, passively accepting that they were late, etc...

3. *Really evaluate each option for solving the problem.*

One way to do this is to ask the client to think deeply about the positives and negatives of each option. For example, if they get angry they may get some short term satisfaction (positive) but the negative is that anger may make the situation worse.

In this stage, it is important for the client to evaluate properly each option that they have thought about.

4. *Seek a sensible resolution action from the options by comparing the different possible consequences.*

Consider the negatives and positives of each option and then promote the client to act in a manner which best fulfils the client's needs. This is where personal responsibility comes into play. Make a decision based on negatives outweighing the positives and, chances are, it will not be the best decision.

5. *The client then acts on the decision they made.*

My experience has also shown that it is often young people with high self-esteem, not low self-esteem, who take drugs experimentally. In turn, however, low self-esteem tends to correlate proportionately to significant and dependent drug use. With this in mind, the practitioner may need to look at the core beliefs of those with high self-esteem. This will be looked at later in this book.

What about boredom and its link to substance misuse? Boredom tends to be a large factor in heavy drug use for youths as well as adults. They may even justify their behaviour by saying: "I need it to relax," even if the drug did not fulfil that actual intention. As a practitioner you will need to challenge this by looking at other ways a client has dealt with any issue (such as relaxation) without using substances.

From understanding these issues, it would be reasonable to make an assumption that by increasing an individual's knowledge and enhancing their decision making skills – you should see a positive impact on reducing substance misuse. It is also reasonable to expect that by doing this you may alter the individual's pattern of use and reduce the many dangerous consumption methods linked to it. For example, by educating users about the risks of sharing needles, you will reduce the risk of them catching possible harmful diseases. This type of strategy has now been defined as a *harm reduction* approach. To the general public, this action may not seem appropriate to reducing drug use, but as practitioners we recognise that individuals will stop using drugs when they are cognitively ready to do so. In the meantime, we can only minimise the risks to themselves and the public. In essence, we must give clients individual choice and minimise the risks associated with possible negative behaviours.

In summary, it is my view that the educational approach and the harm reduction approach can assist in reducing the likelihood of individuals misusing illegal or legal substances. Equipping a client with knowledge and an understanding of substances, and helping them to develop a range of skills can assist in pro-actively asserting this knowledge. By helping the individual develop their own attitudes, we will increase their self-efficacy.

Specific Interventions

As seen above, in the UK, there appear to be two clear strategies for addressing substance misuse. These are the educational approach and harm reduction approach. Some specific strategies turn out to be more structured than others and some may involve the practitioner assessing their client's needs and tailoring a programme from materials they can find. In contrast, there are also pre-planned and scripted interventions such as the OSAP programme referenced earlier. And it is within these well scripted programmes and controlled interventions (or equivalent) that you will find higher success rates for reductions in usage.

Ways of Working with Alcohol and Drug Users

Practically speaking, you should always make an assessment of the individual's use and the harm related to it. Should that person have low level needs (tier 1) then brief advice and support can be given. Should the client have more significant needs then you should always seek support from experts in this field. Do not take this area on by yourself. Mistakes can be fatal.

Always use general community based organisations when possible. This will not only relieve pressure on you (as owner of the problem) but it will also re-integrate the individual back into the community which can be especially fruitful for those who serve long-term prison sentences.

For individuals who leave custody - always plan for their release. The first 24 hours is critical and during this time it is likely that dependant drug or alcohol users will lapse if they do not have support. The temptation tends to be too great. In these circumstances, the dependant client's drug or alcohol use can lead to fatalities. Why? Before going into custody, the individual would have built up a tolerance to any specific substance, and when they are released they assume that this is the amount that they need again, leading to a potential overdose. Planning, transport, general support and resettlement are therefore hugely important in these situations.

On a smaller scale, and with regards to generic interventions (either on a one-to-one basis or within a group setting) you can ensure that you achieve your targets if you outline the *objectives* of any given intervention and session. This will assist any form of evaluation from either the participant or your organisation. It will also prevent the practitioner from going off at a tangent, depending on the offenders they happen to be working with at that time.

The Link between Alcohol and Drugs

In this section I will explore the link between alcohol and drugs. Here, I intend to highlight the ways in which these two substances interact and the consequences they have on clients.

Alcohol, generally, is a potent central nervous system depressant. This means that it slows the body down. A combination of alcohol with drugs can have unpredictable and potentially dangerous effects. In some circumstances the use of alcohol with other depressants (drugs) such as heroin, can lead to death. Furthermore, if alcohol is used in conjunction with stimulant drugs it can lead to what I call a 'false sense of sobriety'. This means that an individual may think that they are alert, may feel that they are alert, but in fact are not.

Alcohol, depressants and benzodiazepines

When alcohol mixes with depressants or benzodiazepines like heroin, it intensifies the effects of the drugs by increasing the absorption rate of the body. As a result of this, the client will have impaired co-ordination, possible memory loss, and overall sedation. As a practitioner, you should be aware of the risks that this can lead to because the user may be unaware of being affected in this manner. A good example would be where the client feels that they are able to perform daily tasks such as driving, but given their reaction time being impaired, this could cause significant injury to the public. Your job is to educate them about the effects I have described. Furthermore, a combination of alcohol and depressant drugs may cause respiratory or cardiac function problems.

Alcohol and stimulant drugs

The combination of alcohol and stimulants may cause temporary arousal, which is the desired effect, but overall it will reduce the performance of psychomotor skills. Frequently, the client will feel significant negative effects which they may refer to as "coming down". This will often cause clients to feel extremely anxious, or in some cases depressed, for a short period of time. Examples of stimulant drugs would include cocaine, caffeine, ecstasy, amphetamines, and even nicotine.

Understanding the effects of the combination of alcohol and drugs will equip the practitioner with the skills needed to foresee and address the issues that the client may present. In order to learn more about this, it is important that, as a form of self-development, you look to any training opportunities your organisation offers. Additionally, you may wish to research sites such as that of the World Health Organisation as a short term measure.

The Environment and Substance Abuse

I am now going to ask you, the reader, to change everything in your life. This includes; changing your job, your housing, your circle of friends and the way you think about life. Please, really think and reflect on this point because, in effect, that is almost the same as what addicts will be required to do depending on what model you use.

Addiction can become a way of life for some offenders. In some cases, it really does feel as though it is 'the only way they know how'. As such, changing these habits can be a colossal mountain to tackle for both the professional and the client.

In my experience, when confronted with the challenge of working with an offender who has a severe dependency on drugs or alcohol, helping them see that there is another way of life away from substance abuse – and what they can achieve - is important. However the tricky part is to get them to see it for themselves. In order to do this, you will have to use your MI skills to help them see that they can cope without drugs or alcohol. Here use building discrepancies. For example, you could ask: "What other ways have you coped with stress before, without using drugs?" followed by: "It sounds like you do not have to always use drugs to cope with stress."

Then perhaps do a cost benefit analysis (discussed in the next chapter) on which friends in their life are positive and which are negative. Go through each one. Following this, apply the relapse prevention plan to their life. Again this is discussed in the next chapter.

When considering peer group influences, one useful exercise is to draw a circle in the middle of a piece of paper that represents the client. Then ask them to write the names of those closest and important to them outside but close to this circle. Next, get the client to write the initials of all the people that they surround themselves with. But this time ask the client to place them close to them on the paper if they are considered "good friends" and away from the circle if not so important. During this exercise it may be worthwhile having a discussion on positive and negative friends. To do this, you will need to consider "What makes a good friend?" The purpose of this exercise is to help the offender consider who truly is a positive impact and important in their life. If they want to make changes, then they will need to invest more time on those closest and important to them. Often, when reflecting on the above exercise, you will find that those who encourage the offender to use substances are furthest away from the circle.

When considering environmental impacts on substance abuse. You will need to look at every offender on their own merits. Then, with that specific offender, you will need to consider their own unique lifestyle patterns. Have a discussion with the offender to see which parts of their lifestyle (if any) they and you feel are possibly linked to their offending behaviour. From this, you will need to tailor-make an intervention plan that seeks to address these problems. But remember - make it SMART!

Summary

When addressing substance misuse you should always try to keep the knowledge I have shared with you in this chapter at the forefront of your working mind. While this is basic knowledge, it will provide you with the foundations needed to start to address these issues.

Chapter 3

When addressing substance misuse, always seek support and get advice where needed. Also understand that change is down to the individual not you. You can assist clients with effective planning and support, but you cannot *do the changing* for them. Expect that on the path to addressing substance misuse the client may very well lapse. It is therefore important that you, as the practitioner, help the client regain focus and get back onto the cycle of change.

Despite the limitations of the educational approach, it is my view that practitioners should educate where possible. After all, knowledge is power, and your role is to help clients make more informed choices. This applies both to young people and adults. The recognition that behaviour has consequences is a fundamental principle of society today and we should promote this on a consistent basis.

In the next chapter, I will explore how practitioners can reduce the risk of domestic abuse and violent offenders committing crime. I will address these separately as they require different forms of interventions.

4

Working with Domestic Abuse

What is domestic abuse? How can we tackle it? Are there any common behaviours and risk factors when working with such offenders that we need to be aware of? In this chapter I will attempt to answer these questions.

Working in the area of domestic abuse poses many difficult challenges. I, for one, have found it one of the most difficult areas to work in. This is especially so when working with male perpetrators of domestic abuse towards women because they tend to hold many distorted beliefs. Some of these can include attitudes and beliefs about 'male privileges' such as "The man is the king of the castle," and as such, they can believe that all other men feel generally the same. Therefore, when they see me, another male - they feel as though I must have the same beliefs and that they can collude with me. So, in order for me to work with this type of offending, I adopted prompts in my own mind about what I am trying to achieve. I call them 'the prerequisites' for working with offenders.

Before I continue any further, it is worthwhile identifying that while I acknowledge that domestic abuse occurs across the whole spectrum of different relationships with different sexual orientations, my focus here will be on men and young males who offend against women. More specifically, I will be looking at my interpretation of how to address offending in line with the Probation Service's processes. This is purely because this is where my expertise lies.

After some discussion about prerequisites I will shift my attention briefly to the journey an individual takes in the adult Criminal Justice System (CJS) after being convicted of an offence which is related to domestic abuse. Then I shall focus my attention on how best to assess risk - based on my own experience.

Chapter 4

Throughout this chapter, I will reference different authors that I feel will help give practitioners a more holistic understanding of the risk factors linked with domestic abuse. Research findings from these authors are also useful here in that many of the current risk assessments and interventions are based on their studies.

When considering domestic abuse, it is important to point out that domestic abuse *is not* a specific criminal offence and that there is no *statutory definition* of it. The phrase "domestic abuse" is a general term used to describe a range of abusive behaviours, which may be criminal or non-criminal. This therefore means that the notion of abuse is different to the concept of criminal.

There are numerous definitions, from different sources, of what domestic abuse is, but the definition used by the Probation Service up until September 2012 was the 'cross-government' definition, based on that developed by the Association of Chief Police Officers. It is:

"Any incident of threatening behaviour, violence or abuse (psychological, physical, sexual, financial or emotional) between adults, who are or have been intimate partners or family members, regardless of gender or sexuality."

This definition incorporates abuse between family members aged 18 years old and over as well as between adults who are, or were, intimate partners whether in same-sex or heterosexual relationships. It also includes abuse that may result from the actions (criminal or non-criminal abusive behaviour) taken by the members of a family to protect the perceived standing of the family within the community, as well as forced marriage and female genital mutilation.

Currently however, at the time of writing, this definition is now being extended further by the government. The new definition of domestic abuse from the Home Office (2012) now states that it is:

"Any incident or pattern of incidents of controlling, coercive or threatening behaviour, violence or abuse between those aged 16 or over who are or have been intimate partners or family members regardless of gender or sexuality. This can encompass but is not limited to the following types of abuse:

- *psychological*
- *physical*
- *sexual*
- *financial*
- *emotional*

Controlling behaviour being: *"a range of acts designed to make a person subordinate and/or dependent by isolating them from sources of support, exploiting their resources and capacities for personal gain, depriving them of the means needed for independence, resistance and escape and regulating their everyday behaviour."* Coercive behaviour being: *"an act or a pattern of acts of assault, threats, humiliation and intimidation or other abuse that is used to harm, punish, or frighten their victim."*

This definition, which is not a legal definition, includes so called 'honour' based violence, Female Genital Mutilation (FGM) and forced marriage, and is clear that victims are not confined to one gender or ethnic group.

As you can see, this definition also incorporates 16 and 17 year olds and a wider range of abusive behaviours. Theoretically, therefore, offenders can now be prosecuted for actions such as preventing their partner from having access to the telephone or money. This will almost certainly increase the number of prosecutions at court.

My own working history, when working on domestic abuse cases, has largely focused on the man-towards-a-woman typology, and the application of CBT techniques to male offenders. Therefore, I will concentrate on sharing my knowledge in this area. Additionally, statistically speaking, it is far more probable that you will deal with male perpetrators on a more regular basis should you work within the Criminal Justice System.

To assist in understanding the concepts described in this chapter, I have included some case studies. They include personal accounts of mistakes I have made, alongside success stories. I feel that both types of personal reflection here are important. This profession should always be based on reflective practice and adapting it to the offender's needs as best possible.

In my view, you should always ask yourself:

- What worked well?
- What did not work?
- What can I do next time to be more effective?

It is by questioning and challenging ourselves that we can truly grow as practitioners (and in life generally).

The Prerequisites for Working with Domestic Abuse

It is generally recognised, from a statistical standpoint anyway, that CBT approaches tend to be the most effective for addressing domestic abuse. Domestic abuse CBT programmes, amongst other areas, address a perpetrator's *core belief system* (discussed in chapter five) relating to women, and in particular the male perpetrator's partner. The main focus of these programmes is to get offenders to *"take responsibility for their violence and even for their own change"* (Dobash et al, 1996b).

Understanding the concept of this research, in my mind, is fundamental for working with domestic abuse perpetrators and gives the practitioner a basis for working with offenders in the CJS. Furthermore, should the practitioner follow this focus then they know that they are not deviating far from the aims of treatment.

So my suggestions (and the basis) for working with male domestic abuse perpetrators are twofold:

1. Help perpetrators take responsibility for their offending and behaviour.
2. Help them take ownership of the change process (as discussed in chapter two).

So how do you get an offender to take responsibility for their domestic abusive behaviour? Well, there is no quick fix, but one useful tool that I have used a lot in my own practice is called the cost benefit analysis.

Cost benefit analysis

In the initial chapters of this book, you may have noticed that I have written much about the concept of writing down positives and negatives (such as in a table like below) when faced with a problem that needs a solution. In chapter two, I indicated how this is a useful method when a client does not recognise their current behaviour is a problem or is making bad decisions. In this frame of thinking, the client is said to be in the pre-contemplation stage of the cycle of change and would usually make statements such as "I do not have a problem."

Positives	Negatives

Well, in simplistic terms, writing down the positive and negatives is the widely used CBT tool called a *cost benefit analysis*.

Cost benefit analysis is a very useful tool, and I like to define it (within the realm of addressing offending behaviour) as:

A practical strategy used to help individuals decide if they need to make a change and begin to take responsibility for their behaviour.

There are of course more complex versions of this exercise, as well as more holistic and precise definitions of its purpose. However, for the purpose of this book, the above definition will suffice.

When undertaking this exercise, it is important to remember the relationship building strategies spoken about in chapter two. Remember to explore non-judgementally the client's thoughts, feelings and behavioural gains. If you do not do this, it could lead to a breakdown in the working relationship.

Using the cost benefit exercise in practice

Let us assume that an offender has been sentenced to a Programme Requirement addressing domestic abuse in a group dynamic.

Before going onto the programme, one of the preparatory exercises is for the offender's respective probation officer to help the client to undertake and understand the concept of a cost benefit analysis.

Often, when you undertake this exercise, the offender will respond with "Well there are no positives," for their behaviour. The offender will then go on to list a large number of negatives of abuse.

Just what you want to hear right? Well not exactly! Why do I say this? And why do offenders respond in this way? Well, in my experience, domestic violence perpetrators are often *very* manipulative within all their relationships. Often, the offender will want to convince you, as part of their bid for power and control over you and your session, that there is *no problem at all*. Moreover, they may be trying to convince you that they do not need treatment, that they have a fantastic understanding of their abusive behaviour, and that it is their partner not them that needs the help.

Of course, if we reframe the above scenario, it is good that the client is interacting with you - so use this to your advantage! The more an offender talks, the more opportunity there is for them to develop their own discrepancies in their accounts which you should respond to appropriately. It is when the offender does not want to engage at all that you may struggle with treatment.

When a discrepancy has been developed (see chapter two), move the conversation on and explore how their own behaviour had a 'pay off', no matter how small. Pay offs could be a whole range of individualistic reasons such as:

- "A buzz"
- "Gaining control"
- "Getting what I want"
- "Because it is comfortable and the only way I know how!"

Helping an offender to consciously recognise pay offs can be extremely difficult to achieve. However by doing this, you are not only helping the offender take responsibility but also helping them see that they will need to change because their current actions do not match up with how they 'want to be' (assuming that their goal is a pro social one).

To find pay offs, the practitioner should use a whole range of questioning. Open-ended questioning is often a good tool to use here. Some specific questions can include:

- What happened?
- Describe how you were feeling at the time?
- Thinking about your offence now, tell me about your reasons for committing it?

Tip: Never answer for your client or offender. Silence is okay. Wait for them to respond. They may be thinking and when they do finally talk it may be totally different to what you had expected.

When exploring answers from the offender for the cost benefit exercise, you should try to avoid questions that actually give the offenders any answers. An example of these questions include: "So, did you get her to do what you wanted?" or "Did you get a buzz?" In doing this, more often than not, you will simply get a yes or no response. Should it be a yes, then things may be confusing for you from an analytical standpoint. By this I mean, you may question the validity of your responses. For example, you may ask yourself questions such as: "Is the client saying this to take responsibility?" or "Does the client want the exercise to be over with quickly?" (Remember that these clients are often there involuntarily).

How do we know what we did worked? One way to answer this is to reflect on the exercise using the two prerequisites as reflective questions.

- Did the exercise help the offender to begin to take responsibility for their offending and behaviour?

    Yes - you are getting them to talk about their offence. Once you get an individual talking about an offence, even if it is to a minimal level, you can then begin to explore and seek shifts in their thinking. Doing this will help them take more ownership over their behaviour.

- Did the exercise help the offender begin to take ownership of the change process?

  Yes - you are helping to equip them with the mental 'tools' needed to make changes in their life. Deciding to use them is up to the individual, but if you help equip them with a new thinking skill which they did not use before - they might use it, thus facilitating ownership of the change process.

Tip: When doing the cost benefit analysis exercise, or any exercise for that matter, it is a good idea to give an example of a non-offending related behaviour. For example, one idea is to ask the offender "What in your life would you like to change?" They may give an example such as wanting to stop smoking or losing weight. So use such an example first. An offender will generally be more receptive to an exercise if they do not feel threatened by the example.

Once you have the client engaged in the exercise, and you feel that they fully understand the exercise and the concepts behind it, you can then apply it more easily to offending. Additionally, you have now broken down the potential barrier of *not understanding* the exercise and the idea (with this exercise specifically) that there is a 'gain' in all forms of behaviour no matter how short lived.

Before continuing any further with interventions, let's explore the process that an individual will follow when they have been convicted of an offence underpinned by domestic abuse. We will then look at assessments and interventions in turn.

The Process of the CJS

When an adult male is convicted of an offence which is considered to be connected to domestic abuse, that individual will almost certainly be assessed at some point by the Probation Service. That assessment will commonly lead to some form of structured intervention which will usually mean an accredited programme (as discussed in the previous chapters). An example of commonly used accredited programmes for adult male offenders is the Integrated Domestic Abuse Programme (IDAP) or the Community Domestic Violence Programme (CDVP). Here I shall explore the CDVP programme.

The Community Domestic Violence Programme is a programme designed to reduce a heterosexual relationship offender's risk of re-offending against his partner. It is aimed towards adult male perpetrators, and it attempts to reduce the offender's risk by:

- Increasing the offender's awareness of the consequences of their abusive behaviour.
- Increasing the male perpetrator's ability to respond to their partner in a non-abusive manner.
- Increasing the offender's ability to change abusive and destructive beliefs about themselves, the world around them, and their partner.
- Increasing the adult male perpetrator's ability to empathise with his victim(s).
- Increasing the offender's ability to identify situations of risk and how to manage them. For example, a high risk situation could be coming home tired after work and the house being untidy. If this upsets the perpetrator, then this could lead to a violent outburst. The programme would then look at how to cope with these feelings.

The CDVP programme has strict eligibility criteria. It is aimed at adult male offenders who have committed at least one offence which is associated with domestic violence. The victim is required to be female and the offender would have had to have been assessed as being able to learn in a group setting with no unmanaged mental health or substance abuse problems. For example, it would not be possible for programme facilitators to manage a chronic alcoholic (see chapter three) who is not controlling his use.

There are of course other programmes that address domestic abuse, but the name of these programmes will depend on where the offender is situated in the country. However, generally speaking, all programmes used within the Criminal Justice System tend to be based around CBT.

Assessment for Programmes

Assessments for these programmes will usually occur at the Pre-Sentence Report (PSR) stage (discussed in chapter one) and, as such, the adult male perpetrator may be sentenced to a community sanction which involves a programme. For example, an individual who may be sentenced for an offence of common assault against his wife could receive a sentence called a *community order* with a requirement to undertake the CDVP programme. Good practice usually stipulates that these community orders should be around 24 months long and also involve a supervision requirement (one-to-one sessions) of equal length. This is to help prepare the individual for the programme, manage their risk, and support them when they complete it.

Tip: Good practice points towards professionals (probation officers in this case) meeting with the offender at least monthly while the offender is on a programme.

The assessment process for these offenders is important. It is here that I would like to point out the importance and significance of a good assessment. It is my belief that by getting an individual's risk assessment right you are pretty much halfway to an effective intervention.

To undertake an assessment, the practitioner should draw from a number of different tools and have a sound knowledge of the factors that influence domestic abusive behaviour. The practitioner may therefore use the OASys (Offender Assessment System) risk assessment tool, but in combination with a more specific tool focused on the abusive behaviour. A good example of a specific risk assessment tool used here to inform the generic risk assessment tool (OASys) is the Spousal Assault Risk Assessment (SARA). This will be discussed in more detail later.

Assessment of Domestic Abuse, Challenges and Key Questions

An offender is usually assessed for interventions offered by the Probation Service via the aforementioned PSR. This is where the assessor (the probation officer) will discuss the offender's offence, their attitude towards it, their background and future aspirations, and then make a judgement on that individual's suitability for interventions such as programmes. The practitioner may even talk over the case with a treatment manager. A treatment manager being: *an individual who supports, monitors and gives advice to those who facilitate interventions in a programme or one to one setting. They will also support practitioners who refer and prepare their cases onto such programmes.* However, one of the most commonly sought after criteria is 'acceptance' (or at least partial acceptance) of the offence itself, and a willingness to engage in intervention.

A few words on the assessment process here. The two elements above of *acceptance* and *willingness to engage* (in programmes) can be hugely difficult to obtain for a number of reasons. This can be because of factors such as (but not exclusively limited to) guilt, denial, shame, embarrassment or even a desire to manipulate. As such, the scope of intervention options available for the offender will be limited for the courts. Therefore, when denial happens, sentences tend to be ones aimed at punishment rather than rehabilitation. Should this happen, offenders run the risk of going 'untreated'.

Under circumstances where a client demonstrates a lack of responsibility or unwillingness to engage in programmes, a practitioner, during an assessment process, will have two main options:

1. Simply accept that they are not taking responsibility for the offence and do not challenge their views and motivation. You can then continue the assessment by obtaining further disclosure for information to inform the risk assessment. Or...

2. Attempt to make the assessment process part of a therapeutic treatment environment, and challenge the perpetrator's thinking to obtain some shift in their respective attitudes.

During the Pre-Sentence Report phase, I believe it is best practice that the practitioner should seek (at least to a limited degree) to work in a therapeutic manner and challenge the attitudes, beliefs and the values of their client to see if their perceptions can be shifted during the assessment process.

In turn, remember that *an assessment is an analysis, not a description*. Descriptions of offences and accounts can simply be obtained from police records.

When undertaking an analysis of an offender's behaviour, a client can display an unwillingness to accept responsibility for the domestic abusive behaviour (denial) - here it is important to recognise how denial can come in many forms, from partial denial of the offence through to absolute full blown denial. An example of partial denial may be when the offender states something along the lines of: "I did hit her but it was not as hard as she made out and not where she said I hit her." Often with full blown denial, a client will offer statements such as "It never happened at all."

In my experience, if someone categorically states that "I was not there, it did not happen and I know nothing about it," (full blown denial) I would argue that should the rest of the interview follow the same unproductive route - then it is unlikely that the client will be suitable for treatment. I have found that offenders should want to change at least some element(s) of their life to move away from offending behaviour. Should the client be anywhere else along the spectrum of denial (partial to full acceptance), then I believe that treatment is at least possible.

With partial denial, you can begin to build up discrepancies in what the client is saying and then challenge their accounts. It is important however that you should not argue with clients but simply get them to try to clarify their accounts at various points during the interview and treatment (e.g. the Pre-Sentence Report stage, start of sentence, and various other points during the duration of their sentence). You will often see more detail added to each account as they accept more responsibility and you can use changes in their accounts to build discrepancies.

Looking at a perpetrator's willingness to engage in interventions such as accredited programmes, the practitioner will need to consider and make the client aware of the practical implications of taking part. For example, the timing of the sessions, the idea that it may be within a group setting, that they will have to participate in the programme and discuss their offence, and finally that the victim of the offence will be informed of their participation and progression. When discussing this last point, the client may often put up additional resistance, however the practitioner should also make it clear that the victim will (naturally) not be able to obtain information of what is covered or specifically discussed in the programmes. Victims will be informed that clients have engaged in treatment and also offered support by a separate worker.

When an offender agrees to take part in a domestic violence offending behaviour programme, an agreement (or contract) to participate should be completed and signed during the PSR interview. This is both a test of their commitment, and makes any breach of their community based order easier to deal with should they then refuse to engage after being sentenced, or if they present insurmountable barriers to their engagement which had not been highlighted earlier.

Getting the client to consider an intervention as an option can be a big ask. The manner by which the practitioner 'sells' the programme to the client is what makes the difference at assessment stage. Quite simply, making it seem like a highly positive step in the right direction for change, can 'rub off' on clients in the right way.

Tip: Do not make promises that any programme will change the offender; rather explain that it can give them the tools to assist change - to make a difference.

Many current practicing officers (and the public to some degree) may argue that the practitioner should not be trying to 'sell the programme' to clients and that they should want to do it themselves without assistance. However, if I asked/told you the reader, if you smoke, to go on a programme with ten strangers to stop smoking, I will make an assumption. And that assumption is that you have no real desire to be *judged*; if anything you would appreciate encouragement and motivation to change, not judgement. So why should we not give that encouragement to someone who could potentially put others at risk. Should we just let them get on with it?

To move things on here, I will assume that the offender has been assessed as being suitable for an intervention. As such, they have also been sentenced to an intervention which incorporates a programme such as CDVP or equivalent.

Further Assessment and Preparatory Work

Following sentencing, I feel that it is best practice that a further assessment be undertaken by a practitioner for the suitability of that adult male perpetrator for any intervention (not just CDVP). Why? Because, as discussed in previous chapters, a client can shift their attitude towards the intervention they previously expressed a high level of motivation to engage with. This is often as a result of 'playing the game'. In other words, before sentencing the perpetrator appeared motivated because he believed this attitude would benefit his case. Now that the sanction has been put in place – he can potentially revert to a less enthusiastic outlook. Two considerations need to be made.

1. Is this attitude of the offender something that, after discussing further, you feel you can change as a practitioner?

2. Is this intervention workable now?

Should the intervention be unworkable then the practitioner should seek to take the client back to court to look at ways they could move matters forward, including a possible change to the sentence. This can mean, in extreme cases (e.g. should there be no alternative and if there are high risk issues to the victim) that the client will go into a custodial setting. This is, of course, ultimately up to the court to decide - no matter what the practitioner has recommended in their assessment.

Assuming that the client is still engaged, motivated and at least partially willing then the practitioner should immediately start preparing the offender to take part in the programme. The programme itself will normally be conducted by specialist tutors. In my experience this works well, and you tend to get better results with a worker who is different to the probation officer doing the intervention.

Preparation Work

Preparation work often involves looking (first of all) at the practicalities of attending a programme. More specifically, you will be required to look at obstacles to attendance, such as transport concerns, employment responsibilities, or child care. The practitioner should therefore seek to work with the client to examine how these issues can be resolved. This not only helps build the working relationship but also increases the likelihood of compliance to the programme.

Compliance is, of course, highly important on any intervention programme. One practitioner described it to me as similar to taking antibiotics. He said:

"You have to complete the whole course for it to work properly."

In many ways, this is true of all programmes and types of interventions. They should be done in full, at regular intervals, and monitored with professional support.

Preparation work also involves undertaking several other pieces of work. If these are not completed then managers may prevent an offender from attending any one group. These pre-group work materials (which vary from programme to programme) generally involve materials such as personal accounts of the offence (what the offender says happened), autobiographies (accounts of life history), and various questionnaires that look to quantify and record violent incidents from the past.

From what I have seen, the benefits of doing this work not only assists the offender in becoming familiar with the areas that will be discussed in the programme but also allows the practitioner to build up a more holistic risk assessment of the likelihood that the offender will re-offend again, as well as the risk of harm they may pose to any potential victim.

As a practitioner, and in line with matters related to public protection (which at the time of writing is a priority for the Probation Service), you will be required to ensure that a victim worker is linked to any specific case. In turn, if there are pending risk issues such as on-going animosity toward the partner, you may be required to make a referral to what is known as a Multi Agency Risk Assessment Conference (MARAC). This is where a number of different agencies such as the police, social care, Community Mental Health, voluntary agencies and Probation come together to share information regarding risky cases. Some of the voluntary agencies include workers called Independent Domestic Violence Advisors (IDVAs) and Women's AID. It is also worth noting that the police will often make referrals to MARAC at the time of arrest.

The aim is to assist in supporting any victims at risk, and to assist in managing the offender. MARAC can be highly effective in reducing risks towards victims. MARAC interventions can include: additional one-to-one support for victims, providing panic alarms, assisting victims in moving home, and even moving them out of the area - away from any immediate risk from an offender.

A Caution Surrounding Preparatory Work

When undertaking pre-group work, the practitioner should always look to learn from their previous experiences and always seek to follow up on any information they receive. I will now share with you a story from my own practice where this was highlighted.

I had been allocated the case of William. This was my first domestic abuse case.

William was a 36 year old man who had been in a relationship with a young woman who was 22 years old, for two years. He had just been sentenced to a community based disposal which involved me as his case manager (to see him on a weekly basis) and the accredited programme CDVP. The offence was for an assault against his partner who he remained with throughout the sentence.

We began the pre-group work and William was compliant, open to discussion and always turned up on time. He seemed to talk openly about his past abusive behaviours and how he wanted to change.

William would often ask to take the work home with him so that he could work on it more. I agreed, and the following weeks appeared to be fruitful with the quality of disclosure he gave being high. I was therefore confident that William was ready for the programme. However, during all that time I also felt that something was wrong. I had a strange gut feeling but could not quite put my finger on it. William completed all the pre-group work, I had made all the required referrals to MARAC and the victim's support worker, and addressed all practical issues.

As the start of the programme moved closer, I grew increasingly concerned about the work he had produced even though the quality was great. This was due to differences in how he presented during one-to-one supervision sessions compared to his written work. Nonetheless, I made an assumption that everything was okay and I ignored my intuition which said something was wrong.

A few days before the start of the programme's first session, I received a call from the victim support worker and then later a call from the victim herself. They both told me that when William went home, he would force his partner to complete his pre-group work and make her answer the questions as if *she* was being aggressive towards *him*. He would make her believe and feel that she was the abuser and he was the victim. Often when she tried to challenge him about this, he would assault her and lock her in a room in the house.

Significant work then had to be undertaken to resolve this issue. This included work with the police, the victim support worker, and various other agencies.

The story above was a huge learning point for me. And one which I would like to share with you the reader.

- Firstly, I would argue that you should be cautious when giving perpetrators of domestic abuse work to do at home when they live with their partner. In the worst case scenario - the above can happen.
- Secondly, always ensure you have made the appropriate referrals. It is only through this that William's behaviour came to light and the situation was able to be resolved.
- And finally, look for dissonance between what is being explained and what has been written in the 'homework' by asking questions.

Risk Factors for Male Adult Domestic Abusers

As indicated throughout this chapter, it is my view that if you want to address domestic abuse in an effective manner, the practitioner should have a clear understanding of the evidence and literature of risk factors linked to domestic abuse.

Understanding risk factors provides the practitioner with both a foundation for assessment and also an ability to focus various interventions in critical areas - for example, should an offender show a propensity to become easily stressed by financial difficulty then an intervention can be put in place to address managing stress and also assistance with tackling financial difficulty. Some probation areas may offer specific programmes on these issues, but all probation areas should at the very least be able to make a referral or signpost to an agency that can assist. So, for example, help with money may come from the Citizens Advice Bureau (CAB).

In order to assist in the understanding of the factors related to domestic abuse, I will now list them as I have seen in my own practice. One note of caution: these indicators do not necessarily mean the offender will definitely re-offend. All they do is provide an indication that the likelihood is greater than for someone without such a background. It is up to the practitioner's professional judgement to decide if it is a significant factor related to the risk a particular offender poses.

Age and gender

Research has shown that younger people tend to be at a higher risk of committing domestic abuse within their relationships (Mirrlees-Black, 1999). This will probably increase now given the new definition of domestic abuse in that the minimum offending age has been reduced. For me this research also highlights the question of levels of maturity in offenders. Perhaps, it is that younger offenders have not developed a level of maturity and this affects their ability to deal with relationships appropriately? Or are older offenders more able to make their partners hide the abuse?

Financial difficulties

Many clients tell me: "I'm just really stressed with money," when justifying abuse. Then they go on to blame their respective partners! This may be of course an example of an offender trying to justify their own behaviour by blaming others, or it could be an attempt by the offender to control money. This is known to be a form of abuse in its own right.

However, in my experience, the practitioner should not simply disregard the impact of financial difficulties but should help to address matters alongside treatment by a referral to another supporting agency. Many authors have shown that financial difficulties do link to domestic abuse (Mirrlees-Black, 1999; O'Brien, 1971).

Pregnancy

Yes, pregnancy! Male domestic abuse perpetrators, following months of anguish and upset in their relationships, have walked into my office many times and told me about their renewed sense of security within their relationship due to the news that their respective partner was pregnant. It appears to them as a magic cure; from now on "everything will be different." They "will change," or "have changed," and "nothing like that would ever happen again."

In many ways, while these pronouncements are positive, in that they express a desire to change, they provide often short lived motivation and the reality of the commitment involved eventually kicks in. The stresses of midwife appointments, financial concerns, and more, build up and the pre-existing fractures come back with a vengeance.

When considering pregnancy, there is also the matter of the stress and tensions when other professionals start to get involved. These might include the GP, health visitor, midwife, and Social Care if the family is previously or currently known to them. The male partner might begin to insist that he accompanies his partner to such meetings for fear of disclosure of violent behaviour. This can initially be seen as his being "a caring partner" and needs to be checked out. But be careful, caution should be exercised when undertaking checks in that you do not want to make it too obvious. Otherwise a motivated offender may feel as though they can do no right and so 'give up'.

It is true to say, however, that (at the time of writing) pregnancy has not been identified as a *significant* and *definitive* link associated with domestic abuse. Nonetheless, there is some research to suggest a correlation - where women are at a greater risk of violence from their partner when pregnant (Walby and Myhill, 2000). Practitioners therefore should always try to broach this area carefully and not jump to the conclusion that there is automatically an increase in risk.

Separations and break ups

This is possibly the most common risk factor linked to domestic abuse in my practice. Often my clients tell me that they have struggled to deal with separation and the issues surrounding it; they go on to state that they are "unwilling" to either "let them go" or even "accept" that their partner may have moved on. This in turn, they state, causes them anguish and anxiety. The idea that offenders do not know what their partner is doing, or the idea of not being able to control them anymore, leads to frustration. It is these frustrations that can lead the offender to act on their feelings in a negative way, putting the victim at risk. In some cases, the offender will go to great lengths when consumed by frustration and negative thoughts such as: "Are they with another man?" In these situations, I have seen clients act in all sorts of ways such as stalking and hacking into their partner's social networking profile.

Research findings appear to match my experiences. Mirrlees-Black (1999) looked at British Crime Survey data and found that, generally speaking, women who reported being separated from their male partners, experienced higher levels of domestic abuse. The broad problem of these findings, however, is that they do not categorically show whether violence occurred before or after separation of the relationship. Despite this, if we look to other research, there is evidence to show that this violence is more likely to occur immediately after separation (Hart et al, 1990). This is why it is important to make that referral to the IDVA!

Family roles

Often, the idea of gender roles within a relationship seems to be an important factor for offending behaviour. Some men have often told me that they do not make any decisions in their relationship and, as such, lose their self-esteem and the ability to effectively communicate their needs. Prior to getting to this point, however, they will make claims such as "The man should make all the decisions." Often, these statements tend to mask a fragile sense of self. Research also leans towards this idea. For example, there are some studies which show that levels of violence are higher in relationships where the female partner is dominant in decision making (Giles-Sims, 1983; Straus, 1980). I would suggest therefore that practitioners who assess the family role as being an issue should look at how their client can be more assertive and communicate effectively (see chapter five).

Experience of past abuse

One factor which you may or may not expect to link to domestic abuse is the client's own past experiences of it. This relates to having been physically abused, or simply having witnessed it.

Experiencing abuse: Throughout my career of working with male domestic abuse perpetrators, I have often been told by them that they have experienced some sort of violent or abusive childhood. While this could be seen as an attempt to minimise or justify their own behaviour, there is research to suggest that it is a common factor (Walby and Myhill, 2000). Common disclosure from an offender will be along the lines of: "I can't help it. That was how I have been taught."

Witnessing abuse: Witnessing domestic abuse as a child has indeed also been shown to have some impact on the likelihood of those individuals becoming domestic abuse perpetrators (Rosenbaum and O'Leary, 1981; Straus, 1979).

Looking at both scenarios, it is important that the practitioner is able to help the offender recognise how their past experiences shape or influence their behaviour now. This could be achieved through a *lifeline exercise,* described later, which can be undertaken during one-to-one supervision.

Should any of the above two areas be a significant issue which the offender needs to address, then the practitioner should make an assessment (based on a discussion with the client) as to whether the offender requires additional therapy such as counselling. If this is the case, then the practitioner should complete a referral to the client's GP. The GP will then be able to make a fuller assessment and take things further if needs be.

When asking questions surrounding past abuse, experience has shown me that clients tend to recognise that if we ask questions about their background then we are looking to link past experiences to current behaviour. This can sometimes lead to them closing down and exclaiming: "I wasn't abused as a child if that's what you are saying!" Following this, clients are likely to give very short responses to further questioning.

I would therefore suggest that some tact is used in relation to getting honest disclosure when exploring this area. One exercise which has helped me in the past is the aforementioned *lifeline exercise.* Now here is how I tend to do it:

Lifeline exercise

Step 1. Explain to the client that you are going to explore *if* and *how* their past experiences may have shaped some of their current behaviour(s) and attitudes. Therefore, in order to investigate this, you would like to conduct an exercise called the lifeline exercise.

Step 2. Explain that in this exercise, they (the client) will plot along a line their age and any significant memories *happy* or *sad* that they have. When doing this, they can go back in time to as far as they want or can remember. There is an example illustration below.

Step 3. You (the practitioner) then draw a line across the middle of a sheet of paper. On the far left you plot age: (0 years old on the left, and on the far right you put the client's current age.

Step 4. Explain to the client that you would now like them to recall any *significant* events from their past. They can recall these in any order that they like and these memories can be both happy or sad. *Note:* You may have to explain what *significant* means here; state that this means: *any event that they feel has been an influence or powerful memory in their life.*

Step 5. Now explain that you would like them to plot their first memory on the line. They will need to write down the memory at the appropriate age on the line.

Step 6. Next, give them two colour pens. One *red* and one *blue*. Red represents sad memories and blue happy ones. Ask them to draw a line going up (if it's a happy memory) or down (if it is a sad memory). The length of the line represents how powerful the feeling of happiness or sadness is (again, see the diagram if you are getting lost).

Step 7. Now ask them the following questions for each memory or event: *What happened? How did it happen? Why did it happen? And what thoughts and feelings did they have?* Write this at the top of the line or along the side of it.

Note: It is worth mentioning that you do not have to do all the writing, you can ask the offender to do this. It all depends on their level of motivation and level of literacy.

Step 8. Assuming you have completed all significant memories. You can now have a discussion with the client about *if* and *how* they feel any of these events have shaped any of their current thoughts, feelings and behaviour. *You may both be surprised by the conclusions you find!* For example, an offender may have had many unhappy memories of being left alone and vulnerable as a child, leading to feelings of sadness, fear and anger. Then, as an adult, any situation where their partner (or intimate other) attempts to leave leads to the same feelings flooding back for the offender.

When undertaking this exercise - keep it going until you have finished all memories that the client wishes to talk about. I would also recommend that you explain to the client that this is an exercise you will bring into all sessions in the future and if they want to add any more memories then they can at any time.

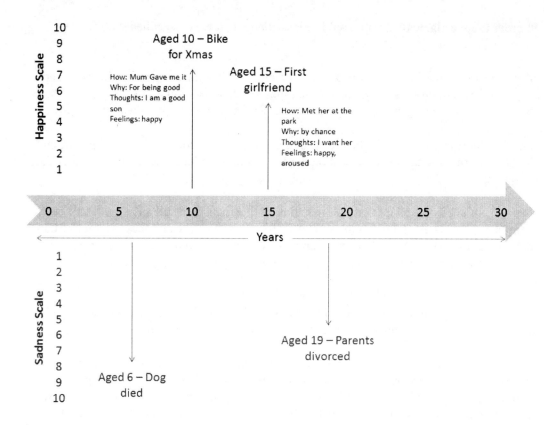

Drug and alcohol abuse

Generally speaking, drug and alcohol abuse is very common when addressing offending behaviour overall. Furthermore, a consistent link has been found between domestic abuse and drugs / alcohol (Dobash and Dobash, 1998).

I would suggest that should you recognise alcohol or drugs as a problem with a client, as well as domestic abuse, then you should seek to address both factors on their own merits.

Generally, I would address the substance misuse first and then address the domestic abuse. My past experiences have indicated that should you be able, at the very least, to get the client to the point of being able to stabilise their substance misuse at a non-problematic level, *then* they should be able to undertake treatment in relation to domestic abuse. A good example of being 'stabilised' is when a client is in the maintenance phase of the cycle of change (see chapter two).

Unemployment

There has been research to suggest that domestic abuse is associated with male unemployment (Howell and Pugliesi, 1998; O'Brien, 1997; Straus et al, 1980). In my own encounters this is certainly common. However, disclosures from my clients have led me to the conclusion that it seems to be the 'secondary effects' of not having employment which are the main problem here. For example, many clients have told me that not being able to provide for their partners and families leads to financial strain, arguments and lack of self-esteem. These, in turn, can assist in the development of domestic abuse incidents. If unemployment is a problem - this should also be worked on alongside treatment. To do this, I would recommend that the practitioner makes a referral to a specialist education advisor (which all Probation Services have) or if not possible, assist in ways to help the client gain employment. This may include helping them develop a CV or registering with job agencies.

In my mind, if you invest a little time here, you will not only help build an effective working relationship, but you are also minimising the risk factor.

Self-esteem

Following on from unemployment, low self-esteem has frequently been reported by clients who have committed domestic abuse offences (Goldstein and Rosenbaum, 1985). O'Brien (1997) indicated that domestic abuse perpetrators (males) have low self-esteem because the man views himself as having a lower status than the woman. This is not exclusively caused by lack of employment, but could be as a result of a number of different factors such as earning a lower income or fewer educational achievements. Addressing self-esteem will be discussed later in this book, but generally speaking, one way to build someone's self-esteem is to help them see their own reasons for success. For example, should they have had a job in the past but not currently, you should help the client see the *qualities* they used to obtain that job. Start off by listing those positive qualities on paper.

Lack of responsibility and general attitude towards offence

When working with clients of domestic abuse, what will become strikingly clear, (probably from the outset) is that the client can often externalise blame for their own violence onto the victim and often to an extreme level. They will repeatedly claim diminished responsibility due to provocation by their partner (Dobash and Dobash, 1979). Common phrases to look out for are: "She knows what buttons to push," or "she pushed my buttons and so I snapped."

Addressing this externalisation can be difficult at times. However, it is important to begin to talk to your offender about defensive statements and blaming others. Help them recognise what they are doing, and break down the frequency of its use. You can do this by enabling them to see for themselves during your discussions that they are using them in their dialogue. You can do so by using reflective listening. For example, you could say something to the effect of (depending on the disclosure): "So what I am hearing from you is that she caused you to act in that manner?" followed by: "Explain to me how she had that level of control over you?"

Evidence has shown that those men who hold patriarchal attitudes and beliefs that spousal abuse is legitimate are more likely to become perpetrators (Dobash et al, 1996a). A clear indicator of this, is when men joke about how hitting women is acceptable in certain situations in their relationships.

Having worked with many men that have these beliefs, I have found it common practice for men to say to me: "You know how it is Jonathan!" They will often try to get the practitioner to collude with their behaviour.

Tip: Stay alert for any occurrence of this and *always* challenge it, but try to do it through reflective listening.

Be careful of the times when you are actively listening and nodding too much; this can be an unintentional signal, non-verbally stated, that this behaviour is acceptable. Also, if you have any on-going professional concerns then make sure that you always discuss your issues with your manager during supervision. This will be discussed in more detail in the final chapter.

There are of course many other factors linked to domestic abuse. However I have attempted to highlight the main ones which you are likely to come across. Others include social isolation, mental illness, and personality disorders.

When considering domestic abuse, it is common that practitioners will come across other factors that influence how we *may* or *may not* work with offenders. For example, religion and culture are sometimes put forward as mitigating circumstances in court as to why some men behave in abusive and violent ways. Perpetrators may justify their actions as a matter of family honour or germane to their religious beliefs. In these circumstances, many offenders firmly believe that these reasons permit them to act in this manner.

Core beliefs can often wrong-foot our work with perpetrators of violence towards women. Sometimes the practitioner may go on to believe that if we challenge this behaviour we might offend religious practice or that we risk being accused of being racist. Remember, however, violence against women is never acceptable and such incidents need to be followed up appropriately. Additionally, there are very few religions which, at their core, approve of violence against another. Especially of the same faith.

Core beliefs are very difficult to challenge so communicate your concerns with your colleagues and take them to your supervision practice sessions.

Working Relationships and Assessment

What I hope to have stressed throughout this chapter is the importance of an accurate risk assessment. Should you be able to obtain this, then you can of course put in place appropriate interventions. There are, however, other elements that the practitioner should also consider before putting any interventions in place.

1. Your relationship with the client: you should seek to have an effective, trusting and professional relationship with your client.

2. Motivation and Hope: the practitioner should always seek to motivate their client when they are not motivated themselves. A lack of hope in that individual will almost definitely lead to a lapse or relapse in their problematic behaviour.

3. Control and Monitoring: the practitioner should ensure that they have good communication with all agencies involved in the management of the case as well as the offender. This includes sharing any important information related to risk and then acting on it.

4. Appropriate Interventions: always ensure that you put in place the right intervention for the right individual. Do not place an individual into a group if they cannot work in group settings. This will set them up to fail.

If you follow these tips I do not believe you will go far wrong. When assessing individuals for intervention, and as discussed earlier, it is important to use specific risk assessment tools to inform the OASys risk assessment. At the time of writing, the most commonly used (evidence-based) assessment is the Spousal Assault Risk Assessment: SARA (Kropp et al, 1995). This is a clinical guide for the assessment of the future risk that men arrested for domestic violence pose to their partners. This SARA risk assessment was itself based on the identification of risk factors from empirical research findings. It is important not to use this risk assessment tool unless you have been specifically trained in it.

Tip: If you are not trained in undertaking the SARA assessment, ask your manager about getting onto a training course. SARA risk assessments help you identify risk factors and if you are in the Probation Service, it can be a useful for a Pre-Sentence Report.

Assuming that the risk assessment is accurate, intervention can now be suggested or applied. Generally, the probation service will use an accredited programme such as CDVP.

Chapter 4

Reflection and Improvement of Practice

It is important that you reflect on when you have been effective. It is also useful to reflect and share information and reflections with co-workers and with management. This will help maintain your own motivation when addressing this difficult subject area. Reflecting on my own practice, I would like to introduce you to my client Sam:

Sam was a 38 year old client, sentenced to CDVP and one-to-one supervision with myself for two years. Sam's offence was common assault against his partner.

Sam, from the onset, appeared remorseful and certain that he needed to make some changes in his life as he did not like who he was "becoming" or even "who he was".

I asked him: "Sam, if you could wave a magic wand, what help would you like me to give you over the next couple of years?" Sam replied immediately: "I want to not get in this situation again, and to learn how to deal with my frustrations within a relationship."

What struck me here were two key factors. Sam recognised that his behaviour was wrong and he recognised that he was becoming frustrated in relationships. In turn his frustration increased the risk of him acting in the manner of the past. Clearly he was motivated to change.

During the forthcoming months, Sam worked hard at engaging in the programme and we spoke on a regular basis about what he learnt and how he could apply it to his life currently. Generally, in my experience, it is important to help clients learn how to apply the skills they learn in programmes to everyday life situations. This way, it becomes more likely for them to apply them in situations of crisis.

Sam completed the programme and we continued to work hard on ensuring that he understood the exercises, their purpose and how to apply them. On one occasion, Sam told me that he did (during his order) become frustrated by his partner. He spoke about having an automatic thought of "I want to hit her" but then began to reflect on the consequences of his behaviour. He stated that he undertook a cost benefit analysis in his head. He came to the conclusion that he would take a "time out" and then go back to help resolve the situation through negotiation which he did successfully and without violence.

Sam told me that it was only through continued work on refreshing what he learnt in the programme that he was able to apply this to his life. He explained that if he had not refreshed his learning, he would have simply forgotten the techniques - despite wanting to make a change in his life.

When considering Sam's story, it is important to point out the following:

- Reflection on successes is important for self-development.
- Reflection on what was not so successful is also important. This way we can seek to learn and improve our practice for next time.
- A client's level of motivation to change is not enough on a standalone basis.
- An offender needs to continuously practice the skills they have been taught to sustain change.

Summary

In this chapter I have highlighted the importance of reflective practice. This applies not only to domestic abuse offending behaviour but all types of offending behaviour. As a practitioner, it is my belief that we should always try to learn from our mistakes and be encouraged by the things we do right. Ultimately, practitioners should stay modest but confident in their belief that they are doing their best and constantly evolving through a willingness to learn new strategies. This can also be achieved through embracing research and learning from others.

Understanding research also assists in both assessment and intervention on a generic basis with regards to offending behaviour as well as domestic abuse. I feel that it is not only the practitioner's responsibility to keep up-to-date with research, but also that of the Probation Service (should you work or want to work in one) to distribute information. *Never assume you know everything, you are always learning or re-learning.*

When working with male domestic abuse perpetrators, it is important that the prerequisites for working with offenders are utilised and always remembered. Again, these are:

- Help the offender take responsibility for their offending and behaviour.
- Help the offender take ownership of the change process.

By doing this, you empower offenders and maintain that all important hope and desire to change.

Chapter 4

In the next chapter, I will be looking at how to address violent offenders. We shall cover some excellent exercises that have been adapted from previous research which will help you equip offenders with the tools needed to stay calm or escape from confrontational situations.

5

Working with Violent Offenders

One way I like to define violent offending (excluding domestic abuse) is when a situation triggers an individual's thoughts and feelings to interact, which then results in a behaviour that has some form of physical or emotional impact on others. Arguably, by learning to control thoughts, feelings (internal processes), or behaviour, we can teach individuals to reduce the likelihood that they will offend or re-offend.

In this chapter, I intend to explore how these internal thinking processes work in specific relation to violent and aggressive behaviour. By understanding how these internal processes operate, the practitioner will benefit not only in assessment and intervention (both on a one-to-one basis and in group settings) but also in the general supervision and management of violent offenders.

In the latter stages of this chapter, we shall examine some relevant research associated with some of the internal factors that I have seen in my own practice - which have been linked to violent offending. Additionally, I will suggest a number of different exercises I often use to tackle these internal factors, should they be a problem with a client.

Learning how to address violent behaviour is critical. However, a practitioner will only ever generally see a client for a small proportion of their week, therefore understanding how to manage violent offenders for the rest of the time (when not seeing them) should be considered of equal importance. For example, how do we know that when a client leaves a session with the practitioner that they will not re-offend? This will be discussed here.

The strategies suggested in this chapter are predominately focused towards the Probation Service and Youth Offending Services but they are also relevant to any other service that addresses violent behaviour from assessment, intervention, or monitoring points of view.

I therefore welcome the ideas in this chapter to be tested with all agencies and their respective clients. Other services that may find these ideas useful are Social Care, the Prison Service, the police, or the voluntary sector which is increasingly working within the Criminal Justice System.

Cognitive Behavioural Therapy and the Cognitive Behavioural Triangle

Understanding how thoughts, feelings and behaviour interact is fundamental to the Cognitive Behavioural approach. Given that this approach is the backbone of current interventions used in the Criminal Justice System, it is critical that practitioners understand it. Now, I am not suggesting that anyone addressing or assessing offending behaviour needs to be an expert in the Cognitive Behavioural approach, but I do believe that all practitioners should (at the very least) have a basic understanding of it. Otherwise, how do practitioners really know the reason or purpose behind what they are doing, other than simply trying to reduce offending behaviour?

In my own experience, and being a visual learner myself, I believe that the relationship between thoughts, feelings and behaviour can be no better understood than through the concept of what is known as the *Cognitive Behavioural Triangle*.

The Cognitive Behavioural Triangle above, shows how thoughts, feelings and behaviour are all connected but separate in their own right. Before continuing, let's define what thoughts, feelings and behaviour are – based on my own understanding:

- Behaviour is a physical action that we can see (if we are able to of course). It is also something that can be controlled (assuming there is no medical condition which prevents this control). An example of a behaviour is walking… or punching.
- A good way to think about thoughts is as an 'internal dialogue' or talking to oneself in one's own mind. These are often sentences or phrases. For example "He is making me angry!" or "I am so happy."
- Feelings can be explained or described as emotions. These are generally one word responses such as sad, happy, angry, or depressed - to name but a few.

When thinking about behaviour, it is important that we recognise how behaviour itself is influenced by our thoughts and feelings which we cannot see - as these two elements happen inside the mind and body. Behaviour happens externally, or *to* the body.

It may be useful at this point to give an example of how the triangle works in relation to violent offending behaviour. Let us assume a client is threatened by another individual. They have the *thought*: "He/she is going to punch me," and "I must punch them first before he/she hits me." This then may result in a *feeling* of fear or anger which in itself is caused by a sudden release of adrenaline in the body. Subsequently, this may result in the client acting out behaviourally and possibly punching the other person. And here we have it, the Cognitive Behavioural Triangle!

Understanding the interactions between thoughts, feelings and behaviour is important not only to practitioners but to offenders as well. In my view, therapy is partially about educating offenders and enabling them to become experts into their own behaviour. To help practitioners achieve this with their offenders, I will suggest an exercise, based around explaining the Cognitive Behavioural Triangle, which I use with my clients. As with any exercise in this book, there are other ways of doing this. However this is how I do it and I will often use this as an introductory exercise when explaining how treatment works.

Before explaining this exercise - it is worth pointing out some common preconceptions and barriers which clients may hold.

When explaining the Cognitive Behavioural Triangle, clients may initially feel patronised. More often than not, clients will tell themselves or even the practitioner, that these ideas are "common sense" and "so simple" that they do not need to know them. Clients may also tell themselves: "this will not help me!"

In order to address this, I always point out the following:

- Yes, some people may see this as common sense (but this is why it works!).
- Yes, the idea is rather simple, but learning to control these elements is difficult and we need to learn how to consciously control them if we want to stop behaving in a negative way. This is better achieved though understanding how elements interact.

I would like to stress at this point that a practitioner should not argue with their clients if they make statements such as the above. Should you argue with a client this will simply 'shut them down' and they may stop responding to you.

Additionally, practitioners should recognise that the client will most likely have barriers to change, and accepting new ideas or ways of thinking is a challenge because they are so used to the way they think. Should this be the case I sometimes explain to the client that it's a bit like creating a new pathway in a field: it's hard to see at the start, but once the path is well trodden in, it's easy to walk down. If this fails, I would simply tell the client that you would like to continue with the exercise as it will lead on to something they will find useful.

Another possible barrier to undertaking this exercise is when clients make comments such as: "I acted without thinking." In part this may be true, or the client may be attempting to minimise their own behaviour. However, putting aside the discussion on minimisation (broached in previous chapters) there are two responses that the practitioner could give to their client to move things along.

- Firstly – the client's behaviour may be so rehearsed from previous experiences that they now 'do act without thinking'. But *at some point* they followed the process described above.
- Secondly, they have simply never picked up on the thoughts they had when they behaved in such a way before (i.e. they failed to consciously attend to those thoughts).

The Cognitive Behavioural Triangle Exercise

The Cognitive Behavioural Triangle exercise is important, and I feel that it is a good place to start with violent offenders from an intervention standpoint. This exercise sets the 'contract' for any session and also gives the client a foundation and purpose for undertaking intervention, as it helps the client to understand the relationships and definitions of thoughts, feelings and behaviour. Here is a methodology I have used in the past:

Step 1. Explain to the client that this triangle forms the basis of the work that you will be undertaking with them to address their violent behaviour. This gives context and purpose to the exercise.

Step 2. Show the client a diagram of the CBT triangle and explain the following:

- Behaviour can always be controlled and is heavily affected by our thoughts and feelings. It does not matter what happens first in relation to thoughts and feelings, just that they interact.
- Explain to the client that if we can change any element of this triangle, then we can change all the other parts too.

Step 3. Explain that, before we explore this further, we will first look to define what thoughts, feelings and behaviour are.

Note: Do not look to over-complicate this but ensure that there is clarity on at least a very basic level. For example, seek to clarify the definitions as follows:

- Thoughts: The things we think about in our mind; e.g. "I am going to hit him."
- Feelings: Emotions that occur inside the mind and body; e.g. "sad, happy, angry."
- Behaviour: an action; e.g. "crying, punching, walking."

To achieve Step 3, ask the offender to define each element using the following format.

- *What is a Thought?* Give an Example.
- *What is a Feeling?* Give an Example.
- *What is a Behaviour?* Give an Example.

Tip: There is value in encouraging an offender to be as honest as possible in what thoughts they have when writing down examples. You may even arguably include swearing if this is part of it. The purpose of verbatim reporting is to increase the validity of the response.

Step 4. Conclude the exercise by explaining how, in order to control violent or aggressive behaviour, we need to understand what thoughts and feelings are behind our actions. Once we do this we can 'catch our thoughts and feelings' when they happen, and learn to manage them in new ways. Learning to 'catch thoughts' is explored in chapter seven when looking at an exercise identifying helpful and unhelpful thoughts. However, until then, it is worth identifying what 'catching thoughts' means. And here, it simply means *recognising* thoughts when we have them. This includes being able to write down any negative (or in this instance violent) thoughts the offender is having.

In the past when I have asked for examples of thoughts, feelings and behaviours - some clients will mix definitions up. There is often confusion between the overlap of

finitions. For example, clients may state that smiling is a feeling, or "I am unhappy" is
eling. In fact, smiling is an action, and "I am unhappy" is a thought. In order to
__dress this it is important to remind the clients that behaviour is something we can see
and which is affected by our thoughts and feelings - which we cannot see.

This exercise generally takes between 10 minutes and 30 minutes. It all depends on how
engaged the client is during the session and their level of understanding of the exercise. I
have found that this basic exercise is a great way to introduce anger management to
clients. It is also applicable to all areas of intervention related to individuals who need to
build on their self-control.

However, while the triangle is useful in understanding how thoughts, feelings and
behaviours interact, it does not explain how to *address* thoughts and feelings to control
behaviour. It only explains that the client needs to do it. So here is one way to progress
this.

The ABC Model

I would like to ask you to reflect back on the definition for violent and aggressive
behaviour in the early part of this chapter. Namely:

*"Violent offending (excluding domestic abuse) is when a situation triggers an
individual's thoughts and feelings to interact, which then results in a behaviour that has
some form of physical or emotional impact on others."*

Notice that within the definition I talk about "a situation" before thoughts and feelings. I
always explain to clients that we cannot really control what happens *around us* and so we
cannot really have any influence on it. This of course assumes that we did not manipulate
the situation to how we wanted it in the first instance. Moving forward I will often use
the scenario of 'someone staring at you in a pub' with clients. It seems common that
young offenders appear to relate to this example well. It demonstrates that the client did
not instigate the other person to act in the manner they did. It was the other person's
decision to stare - not the client's. Therefore we cannot control it.

Once the client understands the idea that we cannot control what happens to us when
other people are in control of a situation, we then refer to these types of situation as
possible *external triggers*. Within the context of this chapter, external triggers can be
defined as: *a specific situation which instigates a violent or aggressive outburst*. Once
the client understands this, practitioners can begin the exercise.

This is how I have used the ABC model in my own practice which is an adaptation of
work undertaken by Tanner and Bail (1989). This is predominately an exercise used for

beating depression (explored in chapter seven) however it can be used here to great effect.

To start I ask the client to list, on a flip chart or A4 paper, all the uncontrollable situations/triggers which have happened to them prior to a violent or aggressive outburst. The practitioner should list these under the heading of **A (Situation)**. For example:

A (Situation)
Someone staring at me in a pub
Someone pushing me
A stranger threatening me

Then ask the client something to the effect of: "Thinking back to when this event happened, what thoughts automatically came into your mind?" Then list all of the thoughts under the heading **B (Automatic Thoughts)**. The client may give their example of a thought as being *"He wants to hit me."*

A (Situation)	B (Automatic Thoughts)
Someone staring at me in a pub	He wants to hit me
	He is going to attack me
	He wants a fight

In this exercise, it is important to list all of the thoughts the client has. This is because all of thoughts will need to be challenged.

Note: Any individual thought on its own may trigger a violent or aggressive outburst.

Once the practitioner has listed all the thoughts, they should then ask the client to list all the **Feelings** these thoughts evoked at the time. Ask the client to rate the feelings in relation to how intense they were on a score out of 100 (100 being the most intense feeling). List all the feelings next to the thoughts. It is also worth highlighting that a client may have more than one feeling for each thought.

A (Situation)	B (Automatic Thoughts)	Feelings
Someone staring at me in a pub	He wants to hit me	Sad (50) Angry (90) Upset (80)
	He is going to attack me	Excited (40)
	He wants a fight	Fear (30)

The next stage is to list the consequences which resulted from the situation, thoughts and feelings. This means looking at what actually happened *at the time of the situation* and possibly afterwards. These should be listed under the heading **C (Consequences)**.

A (Situation)	B (Automatic Thoughts)	Feelings	C (Consequences)
Someone staring at me in a pub	He wants to hit me	Sad (50) Angry (90) Upset (80)	Hit the person
	He is going to attack me	Excited (40)	
	He wants a fight	Fear (30)	

On completing list **C (Consequences)**, the basic elements of the ABC model have been completed. However, the exercise up until this point only allows the participant to *recognise* the situation/triggers, automatic thoughts/feelings and consequences of their violent and aggressive behaviour - in the same way as the cognitive behavioural triangle was used to recognise the interaction between the three components of behaviour, thoughts and feelings.

To begin to assist the client in reducing the likelihood of violent and aggressive behaviour using this exercise, the practitioner should now indicate to the client that they are going to teach them how to manage these thoughts and feelings in order to change the consequences.

To do this, the practitioner should then add further categories alongside the ABC. Each heading should follow these lines: **Replacement Thoughts / Feelings** and **Alternative Consequences**. For example:

C (Consequences)	Replacement Thoughts / Feelings	Alternative Consequences
Hit the person		

The practitioner will then need to ask the client to think about other possible ways they could have interpreted the situation that they had experienced. A useful way to do this is to put the word 'maybe' into it. For example, "maybe he was not looking at me," or "maybe he was jealous of me."

Then ask the client to think about, if this new thought is true, what feelings the thought evokes. List all the new alternative outcomes or consequences! These generally lead to disclosures such as "I would ignore him," or "I would walk away," in the Alternative Consequences list.

The practitioner may then also ask the client to *rate* their feelings. They may have the same rating as before, or the rating may have decreased (which is one of the goals). This shows that the new thoughts have possibly reduced the likelihood of the client acting aggressively. The client may also list new feelings in addition to those they felt before. An example might be "funny" or "happy".

C (Consequences)	Replacement Thoughts / Feelings	Alternative Consequences
Hit the person	Not looking at me - Sad (30) He is jealous - Angry (20) Happy (40)	Ignore him

This then completes the ABC model and ways to replace negative automatic thoughts which result in violent and aggressive behaviour. However, a client will often comment that it is "impossible" for them to sit down and do this exercise when real life happens. As with any new skill ABC takes time to learn and master but once it is mastered it can be done almost automatically. Until that point, my suggestion is for the client to take some 'time out' in trigger situations to try and process thoughts and feelings in this structured way. Time out meaning: *extracting themselves from a situation to calm down when things are becoming heated*. One additional idea is to encourage the offender to use a friend, if it helps, to run through and process the exercise when a trigger situation happens. With this friend (or even probation officer if you are in a supervision session), I would also encourage the idea that the offender reflects on trigger situations. This reflection should be for both what went well, and what did not go so well.

The cognitive behavioural triangle and the ABC exercise are two introductory exercises in which the practitioner can help address violent behaviour with both youth and adult offenders on a one-to-one basis or even in a group setting. In my own practice I have found them particularly useful.

When addressing violent behaviour it is important that a holistic approach is always taken. Whilst it can be tempting to run all the treatments and interventions yourself, practitioners should be realistic about their time and seek to use other resources or relevant CBT based programmes to help reduce the likelihood of a client re-offending. I would also like to stress that the exercises in this book are only ideas that a practitioner can use with their clients. They should not be viewed as being a whole treatment programme in themselves.

With the above in mind, research also suggests that this is best achieved through programmes that have a cognitive behavioural approach (Kemshall, 2000) and one example is the Aggression Replacement Training (ART) programme.

The ART programme is just one of the programmes used in the British Criminal Justice System. However, the frequency of its use is decreasing. This is probably due to financial reasons as, in my experience, this programme can be very costly to deliver. One example of an alternative programme now being used in some areas is the Controlling Anger and Learning to Manage (CALM) programme.

Putting aside their names, these programmes tend to cover more or less the same areas. The ART programme is a group work intervention that looks specifically at training offenders to cope with aggression and violent behaviour. It is structured via three components:

- Teaching social skills
- Moral reasoning
- Anger control

Offenders in the Criminal Justice System can be sentenced to this programme (or an equivalent programme following suitable assessment), and it can be used for both youths and adults of both genders.

Considering the rounded approach with which practitioners should address violent behaviour, intervention (relating to CBT programmes) is only part of the puzzle of rehabilitation and public protection. Hazel Kemshall (2000) has suggested that the effective management of violent offenders is not only about the implementation of CBT programmes but should be combined with intensive supervision, monitoring and enforcement of rules and sanctions. Ways in which to effectively manage offenders will be discussed later in this chapter.

Factors Linked to Violent Offending

Understanding the thoughts and feelings of a violent offender is a difficult task for any practitioner no matter how experienced they might be. However the difference between an experienced practitioner and a not-so-experienced practitioner is knowing where to direct questioning. The skill of questioning comes from a good understanding of knowing what factors are, or can be, linked to violent offending.

In this section, I will be discussing some of the common internal factors linked to an increased likelihood of violent offending. I will also offer the reader ideas in how to address them.

Impulsive behaviour

There is research to suggest that individuals who have a past history of impulsive behaviour have an increased likelihood of violent behaviour (Tardiff, 1984), and in my own practice offenders are often assessed as acting impulsively. Offenders themselves will (as stated earlier in this chapter) also make claims that they acted without thinking. So here are my suggestions to address this.

One way to address matters is by undertaking a lifeline exercise (as discussed in chapter four). Do this, and seek to look at how previous experiences have shaped current aggressive or violent behaviour. Explore this concept with the client in an inquisitive manner, and do not be tempted to jump to conclusions straight away. Try to facilitate a collective discussion which allows you both to come to an understanding and mutual agreement of how previous experiences may have shaped current behaviour. This exercise may take a number of sessions, and it is important that it is not rushed.

Following this exercise, undertake the ABC model exercise discussed earlier and explore situations that lead to negative automatic thoughts and behaviour. By combining the two exercises you are giving the client a fuller understanding of why they acted as they did and then you are giving them a coping skill strategy to use in the future.

Tip: When undertaking a lifeline exercise, perhaps try using a roll of wallpaper to write on. Roll it along the floor and get the clients to move up and down the roll of paper inputting their data. This works especially well with young people and with individuals with Attention Deficit Hyperactivity Disorder (ADHD).

Low self-esteem

I have found that individuals who act aggressively tend to have many negative *core beliefs* about how they see themselves, others, and the world around them. This then leads to the low self-esteem at the root of many of their problems.

Core beliefs are statements we believe to be true in our own mind. One way to understand and recognise what our core beliefs represent is to use a strategy called *the downward arrow technique*. Here is how I do it, which is an adaption of the work by Burns (1990).

Downward Arrow technique

Let us assume that a client (say a teacher by profession) has expressed the thought that he/she is "rubbish" at their job. And this is because (as they explained it) they lost control of their classroom.

The practitioner should then ask them: "What other thoughts does losing control of the classroom evoke for you?" The client makes other statements such as "They do not like me" or "they think I am horrible".

The practitioner should then ask the client to pick the strongest and most powerful thought they have. Let me assume here that the strongest thought they have is: "They do not like me."

The client is then asked one singular question - "What does that mean to you?" - a number of times - until the client reaches a global absolute statement about their own beliefs. Here is an example:

Practitioner – "What does not being liked mean to you?"

Response - "I will not be liked by my students!"

Practitioner – "What does not being liked by your students mean about you?"

Response- "That they will say I am rubbish at my job!"

Practitioner – "What does that mean about you?"

Response - "That they will tell the other teachers that I am rubbish!"

Practitioner – "Well, what does that mean to you?"

Response – "If I am not liked by my students then other teachers will think I am bad at my job!"

And here we have it, the global absolute statement and core belief about themselves - *"If I am not liked by my students, then other teachers will think I am bad at my job!"* One way to recognise core beliefs more clearly is that they tend to start with "If I..."

All negative core beliefs should be challenged. I will discuss some ways to address this on a one-to-one basis in chapter six on working with offenders with emotional problems (section on depression) as the skill is broadly the same. However, it is important that the practitioner helps the client build up evidence to challenge these core beliefs in any way that they can. Here is a suggestion for addressing low self-esteem in a group setting, by undertaking what I call the *Compliment Chair exercise.*

The Compliment Chair

Let's make an assumption that the practitioner is facilitating a group session. The practitioner has a group of offenders in a room and places a chair in the middle of the room, and another chair opposite it.

One offender sits in the chair, and the other individuals are lined up behind the second chair which is facing the client who has sat down. One-by-one each client is asked to sit in the free chair and give the seated offender a compliment. After everyone has done this, all offenders have a go at sitting in the compliment chair.

117

It is worthwhile noting that you do not need to have known the offender for very long to do this exercise. In fact, you can even be relative strangers as then the participants will have to think even harder to give and receive compliments.

This exercise is good on two levels:

1. It helps increase a client's self-esteem through the idea that others are helping to build evidence *against* their low self-esteem by noticing positive things about them which they may have never done before.
2. It allows the recipient to learn how to deal appropriately with taking compliments.

One-to-one exercise

Should you not be within a group setting, I would like to share an additional exercise which helps build a client's self-esteem on a one-to-one basis. Although this exercise may seem simple, it can highly effective.

Warning: before you start, ensure that you have a good working relationship with the client. I do not feel that this exercise is the best choice for the more resistant offender.

Step 1. Firstly, remember that you are trying to build up evidence to disprove the client's internal negative beliefs about themselves.

Step 2. Get hold of an A4 sheet or flip chart paper. At the top of it write something along the lines of "My best qualities and achievements."

Step 3. Ask the participant to tell you all their current and previous achievements. This can be small or large ones. It does not matter, just write them down.

Step 4. Ask the participant to tell you all their best qualities. For example, they care for their family, they are reliable, etc. Again, just keep listing them.

Step 5. List as many qualities and achievements as you can. Help the client if they are struggling. Perhaps give them a compliment and list it yourself. So for example you could say "Well, I think you are a responsible person, you turn up for my appointments, so I am going to put that down as well," - then write it down!

Tip: Remember, as the practitioner, to go prepared to all sessions - especially this one. In my experience, nothing will lower self-esteem more than if you are struggling to give an offender a compliment in this exercise. You could use compliments along the lines of recognition of the completion of previous orders.

Step 6. Next, give them the paper and ask them to read it out to you. Some clients will find this very difficult and may become emotional. However, continue with the exercise and give the client prompts to continue reading. Try and make it light hearted and fun if you can. Should they read out a positive statement about themselves in a mumbling manner, ask them to say it louder with conviction until the whole list is finished.

As stated previously, this exercise can be very effective for some short term results. However, the next step would be to ask the client to go out and find evidence in their day-to-day life to prove any quality about themselves that was listed that they do not believe.

Victim empathy

Historical research has indicated that a lack of empathy for a victim is linked to violent offending and an increased probability of re-offending (Bandura et al, 1975). In my own practice, this certainly appears to be a common characteristic. It is also generally easy to identify, as the client will simply make statements such as "*I do not know or care how they were affected,*" when discussing the consequences of the offence towards victims who they may struggle to see as an actual person.

Tip: Try to remember - showing a lack of victim empathy can be used as a protective mechanism by the offender. Sometimes it can be easier for them to joke about the harm they have caused than to actually accept what damage they have caused.

To address this, I use what is commonly known as a brain storm exercise. Here is one method:

The Brain Storm Exercise

I write the word "Consequences" in the middle of a flip chart, or on A4 paper. I then ask the client a number of questions.

1) How has the *client* been affected by what has happened?

2) How has the *client's family* been affected?

3) How do they think the *victim could have been* affected (even if they think that they have not been)? The words "could have" are important as the practitioner is allowing the client to think in more general terms.

4) How do they think the *victim's family* could have been affected by the offence?

If there are any significant differences with how their family has been affected but not the victim's, you can explore this with them and discuss why!

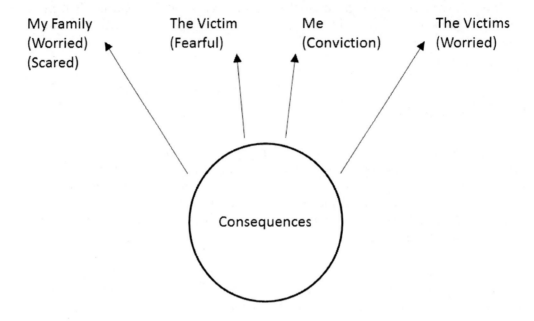

Tip: Use a different coloured pen for the different categories. And if you are working with young people, you may even ask them to draw themselves in the middle of the circle and talk about the consequences that way.

The purpose of this exercise is to get the offender to think about what has happened in more detail and how it has (or may have) affected the victim. It also tries to get the client to relate to the victim.

Tip: If the offender refuses to acknowledge the harm they have caused to the victim, then it is worthwhile asking the client to consider that they are the victim. After this, ask them to consider how an offence (such as the one they committed) would impact on them. Should they then begin to answer this, ask them a follow up question such as: "Why would the victim not feel that way also?"

Lack of remorse

A lack of remorse has been linked to violent offending (Serin, 1996). A common statement from my own experience has been offenders saying things like: "I do not care." It is important that a statement such as this is explored with offenders more deeply, as it may just be a reactionary response because, amongst other reasons, they did not like their sentence. My advice is to ensure, if this statement is true, that there is evidence to back up what the offender is saying. A good example is if they have acted in this manner a number of times prior to the most recent occasion.

Working with many cases of offenders who have shown a lack of remorse, I have also noticed that this tends to relate to an inability to identify with other people's emotions. One way this can be addressed is to facilitate a discussion based on consequences - similar to the brain storm exercise. Before this though, I would undertake a perception exercise to demonstrate how everybody sees things differently and everybody will be affected in some way.

Perception Exercise

With young people, especially those who are visual learners, I would place an object in the middle of the room. This object could be something like a cardboard box with a number '1' on one side and a number '2' on the other. I then sit opposite number 2, and the client sits opposite number 1. I then ask the client to draw what they see, and I do the same. Once finished, we compare the drawings and discuss what we have drawn.

Generally this exercise demonstrates to participants that although we are seeing the same object there are small differences - and it does not mean that what we have not seen is not true.

With the older offender, the above exercise may not work so well. Additionally you may not have the time. So here is another way to undertake this exercise.

Step 1. Ask the offender to describe the room. But make sure *you* sit with your back to the door.

Tip: Keep this humorous and avoid arguments. This is probably best done when you have a good relationship with the offender.

Step 2. Tell the offender that they are "wrong!" (when they describe it) and that "they are making it up" as they identify that there is a door, wall, etc...

Tip: Make sure you do not turn around.

Step 3. Keep commenting that they are wrong. Say: ""There is no door!" until they cotton on to what you are trying to do (because all you can see is what is behind the offender).

Tip: You may need to prompt their understanding of what is happening by saying something to the effect of "There is no door; however there is a window or painting." Obviously it depends on what is in front of you, and behind the offender.

At this point the client generally swivels around and sees what you are looking at. Then discuss.

Managing Violent Offenders

In this section I will look at how and what information to share with other agencies in relation to violent offenders. I will then describe a basic model which has proved useful in my own practice for formulating a plan to manage violent offenders in the community. This model is applicable to any agency that works with this form of offender.

Sharing information is one the most critical elements of learning to manage violent offenders. With this in mind - how do practitioners know what they can and cannot share? This tends to be one of the most common questions that I am asked by professionals and clients.

One way to be sure about what information to share and what not to share (and this should be explained to clients) is to consider the following three questions. These are:

- Does the information received from the client put the client (or others) at risk of harm?
- Does the information received from the client put a child at risk?
- Does the information indicate that they have committed, or are about to commit, an offence?

Should the answer be yes to any of these questions, then this is one of the few times confidentiality should be broken. The professional receiving this information (no matter what organisation they work in) should inform the relevant services. A good example of this idea in practice is when a client says that they are going to kill someone or themselves. The professional will then need to inform the police or any other services working with that person, such as the community mental health team. This may also include relevant formal referrals.

The importance of sharing information between agencies may seem like common sense to some practitioners, but you may be surprised about the difficulties professionals have with knowing what information they can and cannot share about their clients. Furthermore, how much information can they give to outside parties when they receive that urgent call from someone who wants quick information? My best tip is to consider the three questions above and consult with your line manager before responding.

When considering what information to share with other agencies, it is beneficial to consider the impact that sharing information about an offender can have on the working relationship. This was discussed briefly in chapter two, however I would like to consider here what happens when you share information and then the offender seems to 'shut down'.

To answer this, you will need to consider the issues and limitations of the working relationship explored in chapter two. Ultimately, practitioners should make clear that they have a *duty of care*. By explaining this at the start of the working relationship, we are transparent in our intent. Imagine what the relationship would be like if we shared important information behind the offender's back that affects them but said nothing for weeks? Arguably, with a violent offender, this could put the professional at risk.

Putting aside the conflicts that may or may not exist, I have seen some excellent practice with regards to sharing information. This is no better achieved than within the framework of what is known as the Multi Agency Public Protection Arrangement (MAPPA).

MAPPA is the overarching term given for meetings called Multi Agency Risk Management Meetings (MARMMs) which is the title given to meetings held between the leading authorities responsible for public protection - the Police Service, Probation Service and Prison Service. These agencies share information about violent offenders, sex offenders and those who pose a high risk of harm to the public. Other services that may be involved in this forum include Social Care, Community Mental Health Teams, and local authorities. On occasion this may also include services from the voluntary sector if they are relevant to the case. However other services in the voluntary sector will only attend if formally invited to discuss a specific case.

Now, it is not within the remit of this book to discuss how MAPPA works in depth, but it is important to recognise that all offenders who are convicted of a serious violent offence, sex offence, or who are assessed as being a high risk individual will be referred and (pending further assessment) discussed. In MARMM meetings each case is discussed and relevant information is shared before an agreement is reached as how best to manage that respective offender in the community.

Managing and monitoring violent offenders is highly important in terms of public protection, and in many ways I would argue with regards to rehabilitation. When thinking of public protection it should be every practitioner's priority to hold the view that they are in part responsible for ensuring the public is safe from those who have convicted a violent crime.

Chapter 5

When a practitioner works with other agencies to effectively monitor their clients, it helps provide the practitioner with information for a good risk assessment for rehabilitation. This is achieved by verifying information received from the client through these co-operative intelligence channels. I also feel that being able to quantify information, and indicating that you are talking to other agencies about your client, helps to build up the working relationship discussed in chapter two because it makes the client feel that you are taking an interest in them. Additionally, by talking to other agencies, it arguably increases the client's awareness of the consequences of their behaviour. These discussions sometimes will happen whether they like it or not, or if they find it invasive or not, if they continue to offend.

Managing violent offenders is generally the role of the responsible authorities involved in MAPPA and these services will usually formulate or support what is known as *a risk management plan.*

A risk management plan is very simply an *action plan* of 'who does what' in relation to rehabilitating and monitoring the offender. For example, this plan might identify that it is the role of the Probation Service to undertake a specific programme with the client, the police to visit the offender on a regular basis, and social care to ensure that the client's children are safe and provide support to the parents. The structure that the Probation Service works to, in relation to creating these risk management plans, is as follows:

1. *What agencies are involved?* What other agencies are involved in managing this case, for example, is it just the Probation Service?

2. *Existing support for the offender.* This includes both their internal controls; (are they motivated to comply, or do they show remorse?), and external controls (are their families supportive, or have they got another agency to support them with finances, etc?).

3. *Added Measures for specific risks.* Has the court, Probation Service or Police placed additional restrictions on the offender?

4. *Who will undertake what action, and by when.* Here the professional identifies the goals set and when they are likely to be achieved.

5. *Additional Conditions or requirements to manage risk.* This includes activity aimed to address victim security.

6. *Level of contact with the offender.* When, where, who, and how often will professionals see the offender.

7. *Contingency plan.* What do you do if there is an increase in risk?

One of the best ways of starting to formulate a risk management plan is to consider Hazel Kempshall's (2000) model on what she calls the "risk and responsiveness model" which we cover below. In my own practice I have found this work to be of high value and importance. The model helps practitioners to consider what level and type of intervention is required when managing an offender.

The model places offenders under the following categories:

Risk and Responsiveness Model (Hazel Kempshall, 2000)

Note: Responsiveness refers to how well the client engages and complies.

1) *High Responsiveness - Low Risk*. This person needs little intervention as they are motivated to address their own offending behaviour.

2) *High Responsiveness - High Risk*. This person needs intervention because of their high risk nature. As they are willing, and accept the need to change, they should (if eligible) be required to complete a relevant accredited programme.

Tip: Ensure that you regularly undertake as many checks as you can to ensure the offender's level of motivation is genuine.

3) *Low Responsiveness - Low Risk*. Punishment should be the main focus of intervention given that little rehabilitation work is required.

4) *Low Responsiveness - High Risk*. The work with this person should be intensive, as it will require *control mechanisms*; work to increase their motivation, and engage in high level multi-agency work.

Here it is worth mentioning what control mechanisms are. They can be thought of as: *measures that can be put in place to, in effect, contain the risk a client poses*. The availability of these mechanisms can vary from offender to offender depending on what local resources are available locally and what crime the offender has committed. But just to give you an example, when an offender is released from prison, the probation officer can request a number of different conditions known as *licence conditions*. The offender will then need to sign and agree to these before being released otherwise they risk not being let out. An example of licence conditions could be: not to contact the victim or to attend appointments with other services. There are of course many more.

Moving forward, I have found Hazel Kempshall's model useful as it gives practitioners a starting point to think about how to work with any one client. However, this model only works if the assessment of risk is correct.

Summary

In this chapter it is hoped that the reader has begun to recognise the link between thoughts, feelings and behaviour. More specifically it is hoped that the reader has a new or renewed basic understanding of the concept of the Cognitive Behavioural Triangle which has proved so useful and effective in my own practice. I believe that this knowledge will give you a solid grasp at understanding the basics of the cognitive behavioural approach which is the backbone of a majority of commonly used interventions.

Having looked at and understood the ideas and the factors linked to violent offending, I feel that more focus can then be applied in assessment and intervention to areas which require the most attention with clients. This will, in turn, lead to a more cost effective approach and better use of time spent.

Some of the exercises used in this chapter are (of course) basic in nature. However, they do provide structures from which to work from. Practitioners should try to be creative in relation to how they deliver exercises and always focus on the learning style of the client. Do not stick strictly to the script that I have proposed.

When considering the management of violent offenders, I believe that all agency staff across different services recognise that they have, at the very least, some level of responsibility to monitor and share information. With this category of offenders it can be the difference between life and death. In the next chapter, I will be looking at some ideas and the basics of how to address and manage sex offenders.

6

Working with Sex Offenders

Warning note

In my experience, many people in society seem to have very strong feelings and opinions on the topic of *sex offenders*. But what is a sex offender? With regards to this chapter, I will refer to, and define, a sex offender as being: *an individual who has committed and been convicted of a sex crime towards another person* (adult or child). Therefore, this term does not simply mean 'paedophiles' as the common public misconception would appear to suggest.

Importantly, the reader should also be aware that the definition of a sex offender will vary from country to country (as with many other offences) and is influenced greatly by what different cultures and jurisdictions regard as a sex crime.

When considering the possible stereotypes and prejudices of sex offenders, many offenders themselves appear to be cautious of the association and stigma of it should they be convicted of these crimes. So when writing this chapter, I have had to be cautious with regards to the content and how it may impact on those that read it.

As with all the chapters in this book, I have incorporated case studies to highlight points. This chapter is no different. Here I will be describing some true life accounts of cases I have previously managed. When describing these cases, some readers may find the examples disturbing given the nature of the offender's sexually inappropriate behaviours. All such examples have been boxed so that the reader can easily identify them as examples.

It is of course possible to read this chapter without the use of these examples; however, the case studies described will give context.

In this chapter, I do not intend to comprehensively look at how to treat and manage sex offenders. This would probably require a whole book in itself. The aim of this chapter is simple, and its purpose is solely to increase a practitioner's basic knowledge base and confidence in working with this type of client.

To empower the practitioner and build confidence and knowledge, I will begin by describing some of my past experiences of working with sex offenders to highlight what to expect. Additionally, I shall be exploring some of the basic ideas, concepts and exercises practitioners can use with their cases to 'start them off' on the path to effective treatment with the client.

The general nature of the exercises described here means that no matter what professional role or organisation the practitioner is in, with the right training, these exercises can be used as needed. Examples of services that may find this chapter helpful include Social Care, the Probation Service, the Youth Offender Service (YOS), and the Police.

When exploring the beginnings of how to address sex offenders, it is important that I explain what *type* of sex offender I will be looking at. So, in this chapter I will be looking specifically at sex offenders who meet the following criteria: young men or adult males, *contact sex offenders*, and sex offenders who do not have any learning disabilities. Additionally, these offenders will have had to have accepted all, or part, of their sexually inappropriate offending behaviour and would need to have been convicted at court for a sex offence. With regards to what contact sex offenders means, I shall define it as: *those offenders who have used a sexually inappropriate and illegal direct and interpersonal physical exchange or act against another person.*

In my view, the ideas and exercises described in this chapter can be applied to the whole spectrum of sex offence crimes. However, this chapter will only focus on how these exercises can be applied to contact sex offenders whose victims are either adults or children.

Later in this chapter, I will be looking at some of the pertinent factors practitioners can look out for when assessing client needs and then I shall touch upon what additional measures the courts can use to manage sex offenders.

The Mystery of Working with Sex Offenders

In my experience, there appears to be a shroud of mystery when addressing the behaviours of sex offenders from both the public and even some professionals. So let me shed some much needed light here.

You may ask where this shroud of mystery comes from. Well, it appears to stem from the fact that many of the interventions undertaken within organisations such as the Probation Service and YOS are generally performed by specialist agencies, staff or departments, and while these specialists are approachable and provide some support to staff via reports and updates on treatment, the specialists do tend to hold on to the treatment methods and skills employed when working with these offenders.

In my experience, this is through no fault of their own but simply because of how interventions for sex offenders are 'set up' within the Criminal Justice System – where they tend to be separated from mainstream probation and YOS case managers.

Sometimes professionals may like the idea of specialist interventions, as this means not having to think in too great a depth about sex offences. On the flip side, however, this segregation of work can also be disempowering to others who want to work in this field. This includes case managers who actually have more regular contact with sex offenders than those who undertake any intervention. This is where this chapter comes into play and I intend to share and explore some of this specialist knowledge.

Overall, be cautious when working with sex offenders and utilising these skills. Ensure that you have had some form of training in this complex area, and use the exercises alongside support from either management or the specialists mentioned above.

A Starting Point

Experience has shown that any work you complete with a sex offender should really be undertaken alongside a structured intervention such as through accredited programmes. Do not attempt to 'go it alone' or without, at the very least, some form of support.

When you first start to think of addressing sex offenders, do not forget the fundamentals of addressing offending behaviour which is that, in all elements of addressing offending behaviour, positive change can be best achieved through an effective working relationship with the client (see chapter two) and through accurate assessment, appropriate interventions and, of course, building an individual's positive personal motivation for change.

In turn, when considering appropriate interventions, accredited group work programmes can be a very effective option within an order for treatment. An example of an accredited programme is the Sex Offender Treatment Programme (SOTP). The SOTP programme has many variations but generally it helps offenders to develop and understand the *how* and *why* of their sexual offending. The programme also attempts to increase victim awareness which is often a factor related to offending. See why later in this chapter.

SOTP focuses on helping the offender to develop meaningful life goals and new ways of thinking and behaving - away from offending. This in itself is achieved through the use of exercises that have a foundation in Cognition Behavioural Therapy (CBT), some of which will be explored later in this chapter.

The Conversations that You Can Expect to Have

The following conversation is taken from a case I managed some time ago with a 64 year old white male offender who was awaiting sentence after being found guilty for sexual assault. The purpose of this is to give you an insight into what types of conversations you may expect to have with a sex offender.

Offender: "She came on to me. What was I supposed to do? She was always flirting."

Practitioner: "Explain to me what happened."

Offender: "I knew her for ages, she would often come over and we would talk for hours. She understood me… you know?"

Practitioner: "What would you talk about?"

Offender: "All sorts of stuff… mainly fun things like what we like doing, and things like that."

Practitioner: "You said she came on to you, explain that to me?"

Offender: "She would brush my leg, kiss me when I told her to, and hug me all the time."

Practitioner: "Just remind me, how old was she?"

Offender: "Yes, [offender pauses].... she was four. But she was mature for her age!"

Originally, this offender faced a rape charge. However this was reduced to sexual assault for legal reasons which I do not intend to cover here. Now as a reader, let us reflect on the emotions and thoughts this conversation evokes. How does this transcript make you feel? What would you say to that offender next? How would you treat him?

Dealing with offenders such as the one above can evoke strong negative emotions - but these are things you will need to overcome when you work with this type of client.

Conquer and Succeed

Prejudices: Many people with whom I have spoken about sex offenders, inside and outside the Criminal Justice System's professions have, on occasion, made comments such as "lock them up for life," or "castrate them." In truth, these solutions are unrealistic and inhumane.

In my view, should you (the practitioner) be having these reactions then perhaps some reflection is needed with a line manager or colleague you trust. You may even need to reflect on working in this field because one might ask how you will ever effectively make a difference with these clients and build an effective working relationship if you feel the way you do. Working with sex offenders comes with the job and can, in fact, be very rewarding when you achieve positive results.

Tip: Separate the crime from the person and then work with the person to prevent a future crime. The offender is not the offence that they did, but they did commit the behaviour which we disapprove of.

Knowing yourself: This type of offending behaviour can resonate or evoke strong feelings within the practitioner, as described above. Given the nature of the work, the exploratory discussions with offenders may even make some practitioners think about their own sexuality, sexual behaviour, and attitudes.

If this is the case, then it is important to explore your own attitudes with someone you trust. Doing this will help you understand your own standpoints and even fears.

Be non-judgemental: In my view, practitioners should always offer support to any offender, no matter what their offence, in a non-judgemental manner regardless of their own prejudices and negative thoughts (which are, of course, natural to have).

Morals: Practitioners may hear disclosures that bring them to question their own morals. For example, some sex offenders will put up very strong arguments and justifications for their behaviour which could lead the practitioner to think "Well they have a point!" So be strong, and remember these justifications and arguments are all part of working with sex offenders. I will describe and explain what these justifications and arguments are, later in this chapter.

Do not collude: It is important that the practitioner has strong support from their managers and colleagues. Remember that many sex offenders have had years of practice in manipulating people and situations. Therefore, it is important that the practitioner takes some responsibility for talking to their colleagues and managers about working with these offenders. Seeking advice ensures that you are on the right track.

Ensure you get support: In my own practice, I have learnt the hard way how difficult it is to cope with working with sex offenders on my own. What I mean by this is that some sex offenders can enjoy telling the practitioner about their abusive behaviour. The offender can see it as a chance to try to 'abuse the practitioner' especially if the offender obtains the impression that the practitioner is being affected. This is, however, at the extreme end of things, and does not happen all the time. The important message here, though, is about getting support. Also, consider learning to ask yourself (if working with a sex offender): "Is the information I am receiving relevant to managing risk or addressing offending behaviour?" If it is not then ask the offender to stop, and explain why this is not relevant. If there is no satisfactory answer then simply state you are not going to continue with this line of discussion.

I will now give you an example of my own experiences in dealing with an offender who gained sexual gratification from describing their offence. By reading this, I hope that the importance of management oversight and support is emphasised. You can, of course, decide not to read this and continue onto the next section of this chapter.

Frank was being held on remand in custody awaiting sentence for the kidnapping and rape of six children. I had never worked with him previously and my meeting that follows with him would be my first contact.

As part of my role, I was allocated Frank's case and asked to prepare a Pre-Sentence Report for the Crown Court which included an analysis of Frank's offence and the lifestyle factors that led to his offending behaviour.

Frank was 35 years old, white and male. Physically, he was small and skinny in stature with a shaved head. A far cry away from anything that I had preconceived. Historically, he had no previous convictions against him, but did have a record of callouts for domestic abuse towards his former partners - all of whom were his own age. Frank also had no history of substance abuse.

Frank was my first kidnapping and rape case. Generally, it was unusual to get a case with a combination of these offences in such quantity and so I was highly motivated by the prospect of working with such a serious and possibly dangerous individual. After all, this was why I signed up for this role.

The day before meeting Frank, I prepared all my notes having read all the relevant documents provided by the Police. My initial thoughts were *"There is*

---

no way he is going to tell me about what he has done. He is just going to say he does not remember." And as such, I thought I would be battling to get some form of disclosure.

In my interview with Frank, I was shocked from the onset. This was because Frank seemed happy to talk to me about his offending behaviour. He almost seemed to enjoy telling me. He went into great depths to explain to me what he did.

He spoke about having sexual fantasies about young children, but covered it up by being in relationships with women. Sometimes, this would give him a "pathway in". That was how he described it.

He then went on to explain his sexual predispositions. He spoke about how he was interested in children who had not yet reached puberty and then went on to explain in detail what he liked to do to them.

I then asked him about how he would find his victims. He told me that he would follow his victims home from school and then "camp outside for hours or even days" until he "understood" his victims' movements. He would then find an opportunity when they were alone and kidnap his victim.

As I drove home, I visualised what he told me and played out how he would treat his victims in my head. This was usual in the way in which I would revisit offences to help with my analysis. However, this time, I pulled my car over to the side of the road, and sat there in a state of shock. The next thing I knew two hours had passed. I had left the interview in a state of shock, having never heard anything like it before. I felt physically and emotionally drained. For the next few weeks I had nightmares continuously.

During this time, I battled with my thoughts about why this had affected me the way it had. I would think "But I am trained to handle this, I should not be affected by this!" I could not seem to get out of my head the visualisations of the drawings the children made for the police which described the layout of his home and how he assaulted them.

For weeks I battled with what I thought was the onset of depression "How could someone do something like that?" - I thought. This was until I came to the realisation that I needed to talk to someone about it. Finally, I spoke to my manager about what had happened. It was like a weight had been lifted off my shoulders.

The learning points of this story for me and which I would like to share are:

- Always make sure you have clinical supervision (discussed in chapter eight) with a manager on a regular basis.
- Have a debrief with a colleague following all sessions with cases you think you might be affected by.
- Be confident in telling your manager that you do not want to take certain cases and cite your reasons.
- Feel free to stop a session or challenge the client should you think that the client is beginning to enjoy telling you about his abusive behaviour.

Assessment and the Beginnings of Treatment in the CJS

The most common way in which practitioners come into contact with those who commit sexual offences is following a conviction. However, some individuals can come into contact with probationary services following a charge from the police but not a conviction. A good example would be when a young person is on bail for a sex offence. In this situation, young people can be given support in the community by Youth Offending Services.

Additionally, adults can volunteer themselves onto some programmes (delivered by voluntary organisations) following arrest and prior to sentencing. Often these offenders' hope and motivation is for a 'lesser' sentence. They want to show they are making efforts to change and then will not have to do any accredited programme under the management of the Probation Service.

The main services and organisations that tend to undertake assessments and treatment for sex offenders are the Probation Service, Youth Offending Services, Community Mental Health Teams, the Prison Service and voluntary specialist organisations. The Police are also involved heavily in these cases but they are not involved in intervention - more for monitoring, management, surveillance, and support purposes.

In order to undertake assessments for sex offenders, it is important that the practitioner explores the motivation behind the offence and to do this the practitioner must understand the mindset of the offender. A practical way to achieve this is through the application of the following theory which, in itself, could be used to structure questioning.

Chapter 6

Finkelhor and the "Four Preconditions of Abuse"

When working with sex offenders in the Criminal Justice System, there appears to be one dominant model and that is Finkelhor's from 1984. It is a model or method of thinking about sexual offences (or any type of offence) which is *against* a person.

Finkelhor describes his model as the "Four Preconditions of Abuse" and these four conditions are the 'stages' that an offender needs to progress through in order for a sexual offence to take place. These stages are:

1. The Thinking Stage
2. Overcoming Internal Inhibitions or 'Giving Permission'
3. Overcoming External Inhibitions or 'Creating the Opportunity'
4. Overcoming the Victim's Resistance

I will now go on to explain briefly each stage.

1. The Thinking Stage

In the previous chapter on violent behaviour, we explored the idea that all behaviour is preceded by thought at some point (there are exceptions of course including reflex actions such as sneezing). It is therefore equally true that those who have committed sexually abusive behaviour have some form of premeditating thoughts.

Simply speaking, stage one means that people who sexually offend do so because they want to.

By exploring this idea with an offender, you can begin to understand the motivation behind why they committed the offence. This is important both for the accurate assessment of risk and the subsequent accurate assessment for the type of intervention.

Finkelhor suggests that there are three ways in which this motivation and desire to behave can manifest itself.

1. *Deviant sexual arousal* (sexual offending is sexually arousing). This means that offenders will commit an offence of this nature because they are aroused by it. For example, they are aroused by the idea of rape.
2. *Satisfying an emotional need.* This means that offenders are trying to satisfy a need for power, anger expression, etc. This is known as *emotional congruence*.

3. There is *no other source of sexual gratification*. This means that this form of behaviour is the preferred or easiest form of sexual activity available. This is what is referred to as 'blockage'.

2. Overcoming Internal Inhibitions or 'Giving Permission'

This is based on the assumption that all sex offenders know that the offences they commit are wrong in some way. However, the degree to which they are aware of this varies from person to person.

In order to overcome the knowledge that this behaviour is wrong, the offender will use a number of thoughts which are known as *cognitive distortions*. There are many academic ways of defining what this means but in order to keep it simple and easy to remember, within the context of the CJS, I like to define it as: *Overstated and irrational thoughts used to justify and normalise parts of behaviour.*

An example of a cognitive distortion and one which I have commonly heard in my own practice of working with sex offenders is: "It is legal in other countries."

3. Overcoming External Inhibitions or 'Creating the Opportunity'

After the offender has overcome stages one and two, the offender has to create an environment in which they can commit the behaviour. Again, I highlight here that sexual offences do not simply 'just happen'. In fact, sex offenders generally take great care in creating the opportunity to offend. As such, they tend to create an environment which fulfils the following conditions:

- The victim is alone and therefore vulnerable. For example, someone walking alone in a field.
- The offender is unlikely to be seen/caught. They might, for example, be in a relationship with the victim's mother.

Note: Each offence, environment and opportunity tends to be, in some way, unique to that offender.

4. Overcoming the Victim's Resistance

This is the final stage in that the offender overcomes any 'obstacles' put up by the victim in order to commit the offence. This can either be through *immediate force* or the commonly used expression of *grooming*.

Grooming is the term used to describe the method by which an offender overcomes the victim's resistance over time and generally refers to offenders who commit offences against children.

A common strategy which I have seen sex offenders use, is to become involved in a relationship with women who have children. Often the offender becomes an expert at manipulating the victim into acceding to sexual contact through a series of rewards or threats, and punishments. The aim here is for the victim to feel that the sexual behaviour is warranted towards or wanted by them.

The reason Finkelhor's model is discussed is twofold:

- It helps practitioners by offering a structure for assessment and intervention.
- It helps the offender by providing them with insight into their own behaviour and can, in fact, be used as an exercise between the practitioner and offender. By doing this, you also help the offender to take responsibility for the offence and recognise risk factors.

The model for exercise/assessment purposes can be completed at various stages of treatment. However I tend to use it rather promptly - at the start of a sentence. The purpose of this being to help develop motivation to change, an understanding of the client's risk factors and the development of a relapse prevention plan or contingency plan (discussed in chapter five). So, when undertaking this next exercise, consider how the responses you obtain can fit into the relevant sections of the plan. Here is how I do it:

Finkelhor Exercise

I often introduce the client to this exercise by saying that it is something that may help both them and me understand *how* and *why* they have acted in this way. I then explain that by doing this "We can help make sure that this type of behaviour does not happen again" by adding their responses to a relapse prevention plan.

Note: record all answers under the headings Step 1, Step 2, and Step 3.

Step 1. The Thinking Stage:

The practitioner asks and records the offender's responses to the following:

a) What did you think about the victim when you thought of them before the offence happened?
b) What kind of sexual thoughts did you have about the victim before the offence?

This helps the practitioner and offender understand the motivations behind the offence. And remember, be confident when you ask these questions, do not shy away from them or the answers you receive. Expect to hear words such as: masturbation, erection, penis, aroused and fuck a lot.

Tip: If you do not feel comfortable saying these words in a professional setting, practice saying them with a colleague to help build up your confidence.

Step 2. Giving Themselves Permission:

The practitioner asks and records the offender's responses to the following:

a) Reflect back to when the offence happened. What did you say to yourself just before the offence happened?
b) When you think about the offence, what thoughts did you have that encouraged you to act in this way?
c) If your thoughts encouraged you, why do you think they did this?

Step 2 helps identify how the offender gave themselves permission to offend. So if we can identify the thoughts used, we can try to replace the thoughts that encouraged offending with other thoughts - as we did in the ABC model used in chapter five.

Step 3. Creating the Opportunity and Overcoming Resistance:

The practitioner asks and records the offender's responses to the following:

a) Was anyone else there at the time of the offence?
b) How did you get the victim to do what you wanted?
c) Did the victim put up any kind of struggle?

All or some of these questions may be relevant, but here the practitioner and offender are exploring the steps taken and the motivation behind the offence. By identifying the steps taken, the offender can avoid or escape these situations altogether before they happen - to prevent an offence from happening again. For example, if an offender committed an offence in a park, and the offender made it common practice to go for walks in a park, then part of the plan could be to avoid public places - such as parks.

Theory for assessment

Having now explored a methodology that helps practitioners understand the *how and why* individuals act the way they do, it is useful to consider what other contributing factors can lead a sex offender to commit crime in this way.

Here I will look specifically at four contributing factors I have seen with my clients in my own practice. When describing these factors, I will look at some of the relevant research findings and also explain the ways in which I have addressed these factors.

The factors I will look at here are:

- Lifestyle
- Impulsivity
- Victim Empathy
- Personality Traits

Lifestyle

Some research suggests, that those who are convicted of child sex offences are more likely to re-offend if they live a socially isolated lifestyle (West, 1996). I have also seen this with other types of sex offending.

Should this be relevant then the practitioner should help the offender look at features of their lifestyle before the offence took place - which contributed to the lead up to the offence, and why they were socially isolated.

It is important to help the offender see that if the way they conducted themselves before the offence increased their social isolation then they can make changes to move away from that lifestyle. In order to do this, I usually undertake what is known as the old life - new life exercise.

Old Life - New Life

Step 1. The practitioner takes either some flip chart paper or A4 plain paper and draws two large circles. One in red pen representing the old life, and one in blue for the new life. Of course these can be any colours.

Step 2. With the red pen, the practitioner writes down in the red circle all the features and characteristics of the offender's old lifestyle. For example, spending a lot of time alone, getting angry easily, etc.

Step 3. With the blue pen, the practitioner writes down in the blue circle all the things the client wants to change, or wants to be like, or achieve. One way to begin to get responses for this is for the practitioner to ask the client a question along the lines of:

"If you had a magic wand that could change your life and give you everything you want, what would you have or change?"

This is one of my favourite questions as it is applicable to all types of offender when trying to goal set and empowers them to make changes.

Step 4. The practitioner asks the client if there are any behaviours in their old life which they think would be positive to keep and why? The practitioner can also undertake a cost benefit analysis (discussed in chapter 4) to find out if it is really beneficial. The practitioner writes all the positive behaviours in red pen in the blue circle.

Note: Step 4 is important as it is critical to show the offender that not all their old behaviours are negative.

Step 5. The practitioner looks at goal setting, and tries to help the offender outline the steps they need to take in order to achieve their goals. This is likely to require a lot of self-esteem boosting to help the offender feel confident that they can achieve their goals. Increasing self-esteem exercises can be found in chapter five.

From here, the client can hopefully begin to see what behaviours did not help them in their past and what they need to change for the future. It also allows them to recognise any risky situation that they may be currently in. For example, spending a lot of time alone or seeking out particular people or groups to be with.

Impulsivity

Managing impulsive behaviour appears to be an important area in addressing inappropriate sexualised behaviour. Research has shown that sex offenders have a high level of impulsivity (Gurbin, 1999). It is therefore important for offenders to learn about how to manage their behaviour, thoughts and feelings.

In order to do this, I would start to address matters by undertaking the Cognitive Behavioural Triangle exercise discussed in Chapter 5: "Working with Violent Offenders". Once this concept is understood I would move on to the following exercise.

Avoid Cope Escape (ACE)

This is a strategy I use to help address impulsivity with sex offenders. However this exercise is also applicable with anger management and is commonly used in many different accredited programmes. It is known as Avoid Cope and Escape (ACE).

Here is how to do it:

Step 1. The practitioner should explain to the client that in any given situation anyone can control or tackle their own behaviour by either: Avoiding the situation that triggered it, Coping with the situation, or Escaping the situation.

Remember: we cannot control everything that happens to us, but we can control how we behave in response!

Step 2. The practitioner has some discussion with the client by asking them their opinions on the above statement. Here, you are only looking to try to understand the offender's stance on the topic and then extrapolating possible examples of when they walked aware from something, confronted a situation, or avoided it completely. You could ask the offender questions along the lines of: "Tell me an example of when you have not controlled something that has happened to you?"

Step 3. The practitioner then writes the words Avoid, Cope and Escape on the top of a flip chart or A4 paper.

Step 4. The practitioner asks the client to think about as many different practical ways in which they could have Avoided, Coped or Escaped from the situation which led to their offending behaviour.

For example (looking at the boxed dialogue at the beginning of the chapter):

Avoid: Making sure the offender is not at home at times he knows the child plays outside.

Cope: Call a friend when he feels like he wants to approach the child.

Escape: Recognise that he is feeling aroused and go for a run or visit a friend.

Step 5. The practitioner highlights with the client that they can use this strategy whenever they recognise they feel themselves to be in a difficult situation.

Step 6. The practitioner can ask the client which strategies under each heading they are most likely to use, then writes them on a small piece of card - no bigger than a business card you may find in your wallet. Then the practitioner tells the client: "Should you recognise that you are in a difficult situation, just pull out your ACE card and look at ways to handle the situation."

Victim empathy

In my own experience of working with sex offenders, they do not always have a lack of general victim empathy. However, it appears very common that many sex offenders lack an ability to truly empathise with their specific victims. Generally, low victim empathy is thought to be linked to sexual offending and re-offending (Hanson and Harris, 1998). Therefore it is important, as practitioners, that many different methods of addressing this are learnt.

Here is one idea that I use with my cases. I would argue that while it does not directly talk about the 'victim' it helps the offender understand that their behaviour may have been inappropriate and therefore have had some impact on the victim.

There are many ways you can undertake this exercise and it does require some preparation work.

Appropriate / Inappropriate spectrum

Step 1. The practitioner writes on a sheet of flip chart paper, at the top, in three columns, the words fair, unfair, and abusive behaviour.

Step 2. The practitioner makes up around ten small cards, and writes on them different forms of interpersonal behaviour. One behaviour for each card. Examples of these behaviours include: hugging, holding hands, kissing on the first date, touching a woman's breast when you do not know them, hitting a women on the bottom when they walk past, etc.

Step 3. Once the cards are made, and the practitioner is in session, they define what fair, unfair, and abusive behaviour means with the client. Here the practitioner is not aiming for a dictionary definition, but simply an understanding that fair behaviour is consensual, and that unfair and abusive behaviour is not consensual with abusive behaviour having the added element of being illegal.

Step 4. The practitioner places the flip chart on the floor or on a desk. Next they present the cards and read out the behaviours on the cards asking the client to put them under the appropriate header. The practitioner does not ask the client's reasons 'why' just yet.

Step 5. Once all the cards are in place, the practitioner now asks the client to explain their reasons behind why they placed the cards in each category. This exercise should give the client the freedom to move their answers into different categories following a discussion with the practitioner. It is in this discussion that the practitioner challenges any cognitive distortions to help the client see what behaviour is abusive and what is not.

Poor social skills, self-esteem, and assertiveness

Some research has shown that child sex offenders tend to have poor social skills, lack assertiveness, and have low self-esteem (Grubin, 1998). It is therefore important that practitioners recognise whether these factors may be present and then seek to address them.

Many of the methodologies I use to tackle self-esteem can be taken from the next chapter on working with offenders with emotional difficulties. However here is one exercise I use to help individuals build up their self-esteem through assertiveness training.

Before I explore the exercise, I would like to define what I feel assertiveness is. This definition should be explored with the client before the exercise. It is also important that the practitioner helps the client understand that assertiveness can be taught and will help build their self-esteem.

Assertiveness is a balance that acknowledges the rights of others as well as your own. It means being able to stand up for yourself even in the most problematic situations but not turning to aggression. It is, therefore, to have a good sense of self.

Assertiveness

Step 1. The practitioner comes to an understanding with the client about the definition of what assertiveness is. This is then written on the top of a sheet of paper or flip chart.

Step 2. The practitioner explores with the client their rights as a person. The practitioner asks the client what they feel their rights are, and lists them on the same paper or flip chart.

Step 3. The practitioner explores with their client some common rights and values. For example:

- Everyone has the right to say "No".
- You do not need to apologise for everything you say.
- Everyone's thoughts, feelings and needs are just as important as everyone else's.
- You are not responsible for how people respond to your assertiveness.
- Assertiveness is not about you winning. It's about a win-win situation for both parties.
- Other people's opinions count.

Step 4. The practitioner introduces the client to two strategies for being assertive while recognising the above.

a) Using "I statements", tell the offender to take ownership of their own feelings and thoughts in a polite manner. It is okay to use statements such as "I need," or "I want", etc.
b) Introduce *empathetic* assertiveness. This involves introducing the client to recognising how other people feel and uses statements such as "I understand you are having trouble, however…" Note here that it is worthwhile explaining to the client that empathetic means *understanding the feelings and emotions of others*. It does not mean experiencing these feelings and emotions yourself.

Step 5. The practitioner practices the use of these skills with the offender and lists situations where they can be used.

Additional measures to manage Sex Offenders

In my experience, the management of sex offenders in the community, in this country, is second to none. However, like every opinion, there are people out there who will disagree.

The reason I believe the management of sex offenders in this country is so effective, is because when you work with sex offenders in the British Criminal Justice System, offending is nearly always addressed through a multi-agency approach via MAPPA (discussed in chapter 5) and the courts also have additional special measures that can be taken to protect the public.

An additional measure that can be imposed by the court (other than Probation or YOS oversight) is through a provision known as a Sex Offender Prevention Order (SOPO). This can be given alongside a sentence or on a standalone basis.

The SOPO can have a number of requirements attached to it which tend to be based on restricting the offender from doing various things. They can include not contacting certain people or not living in specific places. One of the key parts of a SOPO is that it prevents sex offender behaviours which are specific to their risk factors and which would not otherwise be illegal behaviours (e.g. going to the park). The SOPO is generally overseen by the police and /or Probation Service within the framework of MAPPA.

Some sex offenders will also be required to register with the police on the Sex Offender Register for a certain period of time on a regular basis. On registration, offenders will be required to give the police basic details such as their name, address, date of birth, etc. It can also include details of any vehicle used (as applicable). Furthermore, the offender will most likely receive regular, often ad hoc, visits from the police.

Offenders who are subject to the register must inform the police within three days if there are any changes to their details or if they stay away from their address for a period of time, otherwise they can be arrested and charged. In my experience, offenders often resent having this restriction placed upon them because their registration can be for life.

In recent times some offenders are now able to apply to have their name removed from the register. To date, I have not seen this happen and, in my view, it would prove very difficult for any offender to achieve.

Summary

In reading this chapter it is hoped that some of the mystery surrounding the complexities of working with sex offenders have been broken down and that you have now begun to feel more confident should you be required to work within this field.

Of course, the exercises described here, along with the brief overview of some of the measures used to manage sex offenders, are only a snapshot into the work in this area.

Working with sex offenders is not to be taken lightly, and all practitioners who seek to address these clients should ensure that they are fully supported by management and, where possible, colleagues (see chapter eight). The very nature of the discussions required to be held with clients can test the practitioner's own viewpoints, prejudices and moral compass. But be confident in your own ability.

When addressing sex offenders, it is critical that accurate assessment is undertaken to assess the client's risk factors, as with any type of offender. Also ensure that you look at all the factors related to risk with sex offenders, not simply the ones I have discussed here.

There is always a combination of internal and external factors that lead an offender to act in this way. Be inquisitive and find out what they are. As a prompt, all the areas looked at within Pre-Sentence Reports (see chapter one) are also factors related to risk. For example, employment, accommodation and finances (to name but a few). All will need to be addressed for an effective intervention to take place.

In the next chapter, I will be exploring working with offenders with emotional difficulties and suggesting ways to help them overcome those difficulties.

7

Working with Offenders with Emotional Problems

Depression and Anxiety: two problems I see time and time again in my cases. They often occur together, but can also exist separately in their own rights. In many ways, the commonality of depression in offenders should not be too surprising. Everyone can suffer from depression and anxiety so surely in offenders with complex and difficult backgrounds, wouldn't that make them more prone to it? Food for thought!

Putting aside certain factors linked to depression and anxiety, such as socio-economic elements, I will predominately focus more on how to recognise the signs of depression and anxiety as well as how to tackle them with some useful exercises and tips. These exercises will be useful even if the offender (or the practitioner!) is feeling a little low.

There are many different types of depression but this chapter will not look into all its different forms, nor should it be used as a diagnostic tool. A doctor does the diagnosis. This chapter is only a basic guide from a practitioner's perspective and should only be used as a foundation for practice and to increase confidence in addressing these issues.

What is Depression and Anxiety?

There are many different types of depression, and these are all listed in the Diagnostic and Statistical Manual of Mental Disorders (DSM) used by mental health professionals. However, for the purposes of this book, I will define depression and anxiety in a more accessible way, courtesy of the World Health Organisation and the National Health Service.

The World Health Organisation (WHO) defines depression as:

"A common mental disorder, characterised by sadness, loss of interest of pleasure, feelings of guilt or low self-esteem, disturbed sleep or appetite, feelings of tiredness and poor concentration. Depression can be long lasting or recurrent, subsequently impairing an individual's ability to function at work or school or cope with daily life. At it's most severe, depression can lead to suicide."

And the National Health Service (NHS) defines anxiety as:

"A feeling of unease, such as worry or fear that can be mild or severe... People with generalised anxiety disorders (GAD) find it hard to control worries. Their feelings of anxiety are more constant and often affects their daily life."

The First Port of Call for Depression and Anxiety

Should the practitioner feel, at any time, that their client or even they themselves are depressed or anxious then their first port of call should always be to see (or make a referral to see) a General Practitioner (GP). The GP can then discuss any problems with the individual and make (if required) a referral to a specialist organisation who can help further. These organisations tend to vary from area to area. For example, some areas may have agencies that offer computer aided programmes, telephone counselling or group work programmes before the GP will make a referral for possible individual assessment and counselling from local Community Mental Health Teams (CMHT). All the exercises described in this book can be used in conjunction with outside help, but they should not replace it.

Although many people can think in a negative way, generally the depressed individual appears to be stuck in a cycle. This cycle can last from weeks to months to years. Depressed individuals typically struggle with finding any motivation to change as they cannot see a reason why.

This is how the depression cycle works. Firstly, the depressed individual begins to have negative feelings then they begin to avoid certain situations. Following this, they stop doing things that they like, or once did out of routine. Subsequently, they then begin to feel even worse. And so, the cycle is in motion - creating more negative feelings.

Breaking this depression cycle can be difficult. In order to do this, I will suggest two main methods. This involves changing the way people do things, and changing the way people think about their problems. What I am not going to do is look at changing negative situations into positive ones. This in my experience does not work. This gives false hope and is not SMART (see chapter two). I will suggest strategies that have worked in my own practice.

Before we begin, I would like to point out that I have begun to talk about 'people' and the 'depressive' or 'anxious' person in general. It is my hope that even though this chapter is focused towards *offenders* who suffer from depression and anxiety, it may also prove beneficial for anyone reading this who suffers from low moods. One of my goals here is to help prevent and address the onset of depression and anxiety by demonstrating effective problem solving skills and changing the way we act.

Spotting Anxiety and Depression

In order to address depression and anxiety it is important that people learn how to spot the signs. In many cases, some people may have had it for years and did not even know they had it. Then after diagnosis they eventually say: *"I knew something was wrong, but I just didn't know what it was."* With other people, depression or anxiety may have begun from difficult or upsetting circumstances. Examples include separation from a partner or the death of someone close.

Of course it is natural to feel sad and low from time to time or following events such as those above. However if an individual has prolonged negative feelings which begin to affect their life and which last for longer than a few weeks, then seek advice and assistance from a GP.

In my view, many people fear going to the GP if they have low moods. This is because some people seem to automatically assume that they will be given medication. They also do not want to be labelled as 'depressed'. Many people think there is a stigma to being depressed, as though mental health issues are somehow different or shameful compared to physical health issues. However, going to a GP does not necessarily mean that an individual gets diagnosed as depressed and given medication. In many circumstances, people may simply be offered counselling of some kind. In other cases, the opportunity to talk to a GP is enough to help give the person the push they need to feel better.

If the GP does diagnose a client as suffering from depression then it is probable (certainly in more severe circumstances) that medication will be offered alongside some form of CBT treatment. You may now ask: how do practitioners know when to make a referral for a client to see a GP?

Well the answer is easy - we need to learn to spot the signs. All of us can learn to become more conscious of the signs of depression and anxiety. This is important, as in my experience, people *underestimate* the impact that it has on the depressed individual's life and the lives of those around them. Additionally, if we do not learn to deal with the smaller problems in life, and low moods, then they can build up and eventually they 'kick off' a more prolonged period of depression.

When stuck in the cycle of depression, the depressed individual can in some cases, lose relationships, prospects, their job, and more. And this, in turn, feeds their negative self-fulfilling prophecies and negative attitudes.

Some readers may feel - at this point - that treatment is easy. Simply 'snap out of it' or 'just think positively'. If only it was that easy. For the depressed person, it can feel like something is broken inside them and that brokenness cannot be fixed. And, if they did 'think positively' and did not meet their own expectations subsequently, would that not reinforce their depression? Now, if we believe that depressed individuals have less serotonin in their brain, and with this being the 'happy hormone', is it not like telling an individual with a broken leg to just "get up and run"? Just because you cannot see a problem, it does not mean it is not there.

To give some context of how depression can affect the individual, here is an account from one of my cases of a man called Jack who let some of his problems build up over time. Jack was 28 years old, male, employed full time with a conviction for theft. He wrote for me about the onset of his experience of depression.

"I remember being sat there on the cold hard GP plastic chair. Unable to raise my head to look at the doctor. It was only because my mum had basically dragged me there that I had managed to get out of bed.

I gazed at the floor into nothing like a zombie as the GP asked what she could do for me. The next thing I knew? I burst out into uncontrollable tears. Here I was, a 17 stone bodybuilder, in pieces.

I could not stop thinking about how I had failed as a person. My relationships, my job, my finances. Everything was ruined, and it was all my fault. How could anything get better? I thought I had lost everything. I just wanted to be dead, nothing would get better. My mind was racing, but I could not bring myself to string a sentence together to tell the doctor what was going on in me. Somehow, I was able to mutter the words I could not cope anymore!

The doctor then asked me if I had thought about killing myself. I said yes. She then asked if I had planned to do it. I struggled to respond, but said yes. She asked how? I wondered why she was asking. Did she want tips or something? But I explained how.

I felt sick just talking about it. I just wanted my bed and to curl up and die. After around a further 10 minutes, the doctor signed me off work and gave me a prescription for medication telling me they would not kick in for a few weeks. This did not make me feel any better? I thought that I could not go on like this for another 2 weeks? How can I cope? I have nothing to live for!"

Jack was evidently struggling to cope and function at a level he was previously able to. After a few weeks of being on medication, he begun to believe he could cope with some of the negative feelings and thoughts he had. As such, he was then able to start to address some of his problems by beginning to talk with a mental health professional. For Jack, medication took the "edge off" some of his severe negative feelings and thoughts so that he could take the first steps to recovery. Here is it worth pointing out that although medication is not for everyone Jack was given it because he felt as though he was at his lowest and was not able to cope. Additionally, depression was significantly impacting on his daily functioning.

In order to help people to spot depression as soon as possible, we need to recognise the signs. I will therefore describe many of the common symptoms of depression and anxiety that we may see in offenders. This is by no means an exhaustive list and reading the next section should not be used as a diagnostic tool. It does, however, provide an indication of what to look out for with clients and even ourselves. This list therefore, could be used as a basic form of screening to signpost a client to a GP or a mental health professional.

To help the practitioner identify the signs of depression and anxiety, I will divide up the symptoms into subcategories. These are: common feelings, common body reactions, common thoughts and common behaviours. I will start with symptoms of depression.

Common feelings of depression

Depressive feelings can feel more intense to the depressive compared to those who do not suffer from depression - the 'norm'. Often clients will people feel 'unbearably lonely, sad and upset'. Some will feel guilty over the smallest things, while others will feel guilty for situations that were not their fault.

Common body reaction of depression

In the depressed individual, significant changes can occur in relation to their body's normal level of functioning. The depressed person can feel tired all the time, talk about sleep problems, have changes in appetite, loss of sex drive, and no energy. Many will also have inexplicable aches and pains.

Common behaviours for those with depression

Outward behaviours are typically the most noticeable indicators of depression for the observer and difficult to hide by the depressive. An individual will be tearful, have slowed down reactions, struggle with making decisions, and show a lack of concentration. Often they will resort to alcohol or drugs as a coping strategy and in extreme cases withdraw from others socially whilst using these substances. Some however may not use drugs and alcohol and will simply withdraw from interactions with as many people as they can, loved ones, friends, whomever.

Common thoughts in depression

It seems self-evident that we will only be able to properly identify depression if the depressive tells us or we identify it within ourselves. And we can do this by unearthing people's thoughts about themselves. The depressed individual tends to feel as though a thought is a true fact rather than only a possibility. So, examples of thoughts for a depressed person are:

- "I am inferior or ill"
- "I am going mad"
- "Life is not worth living"
- "I am useless"

In my experience, what seems to be all too common (above and beyond all the symptoms of depression) is the depressed individual's loss of hope. And by this I mean hope in practically anything. For example, people seem to lose all hope of change, hope of finding something better, or even the hope that depression will eventually end. Hope is so important, and if not maintained, the offender (specifically) may lack the motivation to comply with anything - including a sentence following a conviction. One common phrase to look out for here and which I hear time and time again is: "I cannot be bothered to do this or that..."

Often, people with depression also seem to suffer from anxiety. As stated earlier however, anxiety can occur by itself. I will now explore some of the common symptoms here.

Common feelings of anxiety

Those who feel anxious often describe feelings of nervousness in all sorts of unique circumstances. They can also talk about feeling 'on edge' or agitated much of the time. Many feel terrified - terrified of going outside, or terrified of seeing certain people. These feelings tend to quickly sap any confidence that the anxious person has which in turns makes room for 'worry' to kick in. And when I say worry, severely anxious individuals can worry about almost everything. For example, I had one case where the client would sit and talk to me imagining every possible negative outcome of a specific situation, worrying about *all* the bad things that could happen. Even if it was just walking to the shop to buy some milk.

Common body reactions of anxiety

All symptoms of anxiety and depression are horrible for the anxious or depressed person. However, the bodily reaction symptoms of anxiety sufferers tends to provide evidence to the individual that they 'cannot cope' or that they are 'going mad'. When considering physical/bodily reactions, the body can begin to shake, feel dizzy, or even sweat more than usual. Sometimes they feel as though their breathing is affected. Their chest becomes tight and they feel as though they cannot take in enough oxygen. This can leave them feeling sick.

Common behaviour reactions of anxiety

Due to the feelings of anxiety and associated body reactions, the anxious person describes not feeling able to relax no matter how hard they try. That relaxing piece of music that they once responded to – it no longer works. That soothing bath becomes a place where they think about self-harm.

When thinking about anxiety, another sign of an anxious person is that they will seek to avoid the situations that they once thrived in; they avoid anything that they cannot control. The individual who once wanted to lead is now at the back of the line all the time. A good example here, for learning to spot this, is when someone (in this case the client) begins to make many different excuses not to do something or go somewhere - this also appears to the onlooker as being out of character.

Common thoughts of anxiety

Thoughts and feelings can happen at any time and in any order. It does not matter which one comes first, we just need to know that they happen. Anxious thoughts are, of course, often linked to depressive thoughts. The anxious individual feels as though they are losing control and think "If I cannot control myself, how can I control anything?" Often sufferers will then say to themselves that they are "ill" or that: "If I stay here at home - something bad is going to happen!" Then if they consider going outside or doing something that might help them, they start to think "Well if I do that, I will make a fool out of myself."

Changing the Way We Do Things

When we consider the way a depressed and anxious person behaves, we notice that they stop doing things they would normally do. Simple tasks can become a bit like climbing Mount Everest for them. As we saw in the depressive cycle this then makes them feel worse and they slowly try to withdraw from the world. It is therefore important that professionals know what options they can give to the depressed person to help alleviate some of the problems. This is what we shall now explore.

Get active

Okay, should you identify a client suffering from depression (or you feel like you are becoming depressed or feeling down) – it is a good idea to get active. Numerous studies have shown how physical activity can reduce a person's negative feelings. Get up and go do some exercise. Just get up and do something. Anything! Wash the dishes, organise the shed, go for a walk. Or even better, go to the gym! By being active, we release endorphins which help battle depression and which provide relief.

I do appreciate here, that this is easier said than done. When someone has very low motivation, getting active is probably the hardest thing to do - but it is a simple and effective way to combat depression.

When working with offenders, if the idea of getting active seems overwhelming - set the client small achievable SMART goals (see chapter one). In this case, it could simply be "I will walk outside for five minutes every morning for a week," to start.

Tip: It would be beneficial for the professional to source free activities or free gym passes to present to the offender as options they could pursue. Sometimes, actions such as going to the gym may not be financially feasible for a client.

Do the opposite

Fight depression! And do the opposite to what it is telling you to do. This is the case especially when depression is telling you to avoid your commitments or if it is telling you to avoid something you enjoyed previously. Depression will tell the depressive: "You *cannot* do this or that." For example, I had one offender who would say: "I cannot attend my appointments as I get too anxious."

The depressed person needs to do the opposite. This will seem hard. In many cases, it will seem like a colossal effort. However, doing the opposite to what depression tells you is effective for showing the individual that the situation is not as bad as they thought. In the case of the example above, my client eventually came to an appointment and ended the session saying that he had actually "enjoyed it."

Here, as a practitioner, two elements need to be considered. Firstly, the practitioner should try to find out the reasons (thoughts) for a client's behaviour. For example, you will need to consider what thoughts are making the client behave as they are (which from the example above is not attending appointments). Secondly, once the professional knows the reasoning behind any action we can set small goals for the offender to achieve. We shall explore how to record and identify thoughts later in this chapter.

Get out of bed

Many depressives struggle to get out of bed after, ironically, spending the night trying to sleep. Some people fear that if they get out of bed it simply provides another opportunity for them to fail. They deduce in their mind that it is better to lie there and wait for everything to come collapsing down on them.

So here is what I suggest: should anyone be prone to depression or low moods, then they must, and I mean must (!) get out of bed in the morning *as soon as they wake up*. Procrastination in bed for the depressive is a sure fire way for them to start pondering what a 'failure they are.' This is formally known as *ruminating*.

The depressive should get up when they wake up, and *stay out of bed* unless it is to sleep at night. Of course, this does not mean then moving to the sofa and sleeping there. Once up, stay up, and do not be tempted to take naps.

Motivation follows action

One of the most difficult things for a depressed person is to find the motivation to actually implement the behavioural changes I suggest. However, if anyone is to take anything from this chapter then take this saying: "Motivation to do anything will always follow action, and not the other way around."

Motivation follows action. Have you noticed that sometimes, in everyday life, we "cannot be bothered" to do what we think we should do. For example, going to the gym. We will find every excuse possible not to go in our heads. For example, "I am too tired," or "I worked hard at the gym last week, so I can go less this week." Then for whatever reason, we go, and then have the best session we have had in ages and feel great that we actually went. We then decide that we will not only go to the gym all week now but we will also now start to eat more healthily. Sound at all familiar? Action can be a virtuous circle. It leads to positive change.

There are plenty of different examples of motivation following action - however the depressed person struggles here. In order to achieve this change, we need to change our beliefs and challenge negative thoughts. This will be discussed and explored later in this chapter when we identify what *unhelpful thoughts* are, and how to change them using the ABC model.

No one is perfect!

This is about recognising and changing beliefs as the depressed or anxious individual usually has many unrealistic and unhelpful beliefs about themselves, the world, and others. The good thing about beliefs is that they can be changed to anything you want. Finding your beliefs can be found by using the *downward arrow technique* described in chapter five. Then, we can challenge them using the ABC model described later in this chapter.

In reality, no one is perfect. This might sound like a cliché but depressed individuals often do not believe that this is true. They can have huge expectations for themselves and convince themselves of things that are outside rational thoughts. Ironically, some depressed individuals are often the most successful in business - they stay up all hours of the day and work all night until they have achieved their goals because failure is not an option. If they do fail then they simply cannot understand 'why' other than that they are not good enough. A good exercise here is to remind depressed individuals of SMART goal setting. In my mind, you can always spot the people most prone to depression. They are usually the ones that stay late in the office all the time and still appear stressed or spend too much time pondering something.

Get out of your comfort zone

On occasion, the depressed person will not be willing to undertake a certain project to the point of point blank refusal (which can come across as rude, even when they did not intend for it to come out that way). They fear that if they cannot meet their own perfectionist expectations then it is not worth it as it will be just another example of their own failure.

My advice? Remind the depressed person that they are just scared of what they could actually achieve. Staying in one's comfort zone is familiar and easy. They cannot fail there. The depressed person needs to let go of the ideal of perfectionism and remaining in the comfort zone. They need to take on new challenges and experience new things. Just take a few steps towards something new and more motivation will follow.

Routine

You often hear people say: "I hate routine," or "I find routine boring." This is fine for some people; everyone is free to have their own ways after all! However, I would argue that with depressed people (and let's relate back to offenders here) - routine is essential. I recommend that the depressed offender actually sits down every week and plans their week ahead. In CBT lingo – this is called *scheduling*.

Remember to do fun things

Some depressed people stop enjoying things that they used to enjoy, and take no enjoyment from what others do. Often, this will frustrate others and comments such as "You don't like anything do you?" or "What is wrong with you?" are made. The onlooker may actually take the depressive's reticence personally.

You need to explain to the depressed person that this state is only temporary and normal to experience in depression.

When working with depression, it is important to think about what the depressed person liked doing *before* they were depressed or what they want to achieve in the future. This can be achieved through some of the goal setting exercises I suggested in chapter two.

Often, in CBT, the client will be asked to incorporate a number of pleasurable activities into their new daily routine. For offenders it is important that they do not incorporate activities that led them into the Criminal Justice System. So with these individuals it is essential to think of positive non-criminal activities. Anything the client once used to like. One of these activities should be put in the routine every day, alongside all the essential day-to-day activities such as paying the bills. Additionally, the client should be asked to rate how much they expect to enjoy that task before the week starts, and then to score things once again after the event.

Here is how I do it step-by-step. Before you start, you will need a weekly calendar. Simply get an A4 sheet of paper and list the days of the week at the top and then draw three rows representing morning, afternoon, and evening. You may also need to clarify what these times mean with the client. See the following diagram:

	Monday	Tuesday	Wednesday	Thursday	Friday	Saturday	Sunday
Morning							
Afternoon							
Evening							

Now follow these steps:

Step 1. Ask the client to list any activities that they like or liked doing.

Step 2. Ask them to list important things that they need to do. Such as paying bills and so on.

Step 3. Show the client the weekly calendar and separate all the tasks that they need to do across the week. Make sure they are in line with any existing activities/appointments that need to be adhered to.

Step 4. Put a pleasurable activity into each day. This can be the same activity if you only have one - it can also be put in at any time that the client can do it. Morning, afternoon or evening.

Step 5. Ask the client to rate out of ten (ten being very pleasurable) how good they believe the pleasurable activity will make them feel *before* they do it. Record this on the calendar. Then ask the client to record out of ten how happy or pleasurable this activity was *after* they did it. The calendar should end up looking something like this:

	Mon	Tues	Wed	Thurs	Fri	Sat	Sun
Morning	*Go to Job Centre*		*Probation appoint--ment*		*Pay electric*		
Afternoon					*Go to Cinema* Before (5) After (7)		
Evening	*10 min walk* Before (4) After (7)	*10 min walk* Before (4) After (7)	*See Friend* Before (3) After (6)	*10 min walk* Before (4) After (7)		*10 min walk* Before (4) After (7)	*See Friend* Before (3) After (6)

Note: If the client cannot put something into every day, do not worry, just aim for it where possible.

Step 6. Review all the activities for the time period set (in this case a week) in your next session and review whether the activities met the client's pleasurable expectations. You will often find that pleasurable activities were considered more pleasurable than initially thought and recorded.

Often when goal setting or undertaking this exercise with offenders - I like to explain how depression is actually a chance for people to rebuild themselves. It is sometimes a chance for them to find the positive things inside of them that they never knew existed before. And most importantly depression will get better; the depressed person will become stronger as a person. Depression can be a gilt-edged opportunity for the practitioner to facilitate positive change.

Eat well, drink well

Before I look at ways to change the way people think, I would like to talk about the importance of diet in the depressed person. Some depressed people will drink more alcohol or use drugs whilst others will stop eating and have the attitude that they do not want to take anything or eat as they simply want everything to end; eating will only prolong the pain. At the opposite end of the scale, some people will overeat as binge eating will make them feel good for a minute (but ten times worse once they realise what they have done).

So my tip is to think about or talk about ways in which people can eat healthily and not skip meals. It is important to NOT DRINK ALCOHOL or take DRUGS (illegal drugs) when depressed. This is particularly important when an individual has been prescribed medication to help treat their mental health problems. Recreational drugs can upset the effectiveness of prescribed medication and will make the depressive feel worse. Additionally avoid caffeine drinks and drink plenty of water. I knew one individual that would drink so many highly caffeinated energy drinks that it made them *unbearably* anxious. Common sense right?

Changing the Way We Think about Problems

Few depressed people will believe you when you tell them that "Things can get better!" But they really can! However in order to bring about positive change, they will need to make changes in the way they think. They need to learn, as we all do, to bring more balance to their thoughts when they get us down.

In order to do this, they need to learn new skills to change the way they think, they then need to practice them, and keep using them until they become second nature. The skills I will now share help to structure our thoughts. Now, by making 'changes to the way we think', I categorically mean giving a new structure for thoughts for a more balanced viewpoint only. I do not mean giving false hope, or turning negative thoughts into positives (with a magic wand) like some books suggest.

Depressed people, in my experience, seem to lack perspective and rationality when at their lowest ebbs. They can only see the negative and will not settle for more rational viewpoints. And if someone else gives this to them, sometimes this relief will only last a little while and then the depression sufferer will fall back into their own irrational thinking. This structure helps stop that!

So what is this new structure to thinking to help give depressed people (and maybe us) some more balance? Well before I answer this, it is important that we learn to understand our thoughts in more detail. Once we do this, we can change them.

Catching Thoughts

As explored in chapter five, we know that thoughts, feelings and behaviour are all linked. This is illustrated by the Cognitive Behavioural Triangle.

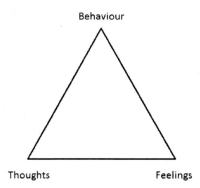

We can also now further divide our thoughts into helpful and unhelpful thoughts.

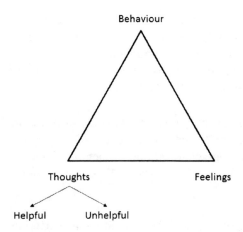

With clients I will often draw a table and ask them to tell me about the thoughts that make them upset, and what thoughts make them feel good. Upsetting thoughts will go in the unhelpful column and good thoughts will go in the helpful column. This is important to do as the client can then learn to catch their negative thoughts

Here is an example of how it is done with the type of thoughts you are looking for:

Unhelpful or upsetting thoughts "Thoughts that make me depressed"	Helpful good thoughts "Thoughts that make me feel good"
I am a failure	I am sometimes good at sport
No one will like me	I can be a helpful son / daughter
I am a bad person	I have lots of qualifications
I cannot cope	This is my first time in trouble
Everything is rubbish	
I will never get better	

When undertaking this exercise, it is unlikely that the client will be able to think of all their unhelpful thoughts in one session. It is therefore useful for the offender to take the exercises away and record additional thoughts throughout the week. It is important to note, however, that when recording these thoughts, they should be written down as many times as they occur. So for example, the depressive may have the thought "I am a failure" on Monday, and it should be written down. They then have it again on Tuesday. Again, it should be written down. And so on.

What the depressive will find is that they often have the same thoughts again and again. The most common unhelpful thoughts we have are our actual core beliefs about ourselves and these unhealthy thoughts are known in CBT as *thinking errors*. Thinking errors have many forms and are quite simply not good for the way we think. We need to be able to identify them before we can tackle them.

On occasion, these thinking errors may pop into the mind as questions. For example, the depressive may have the thought: "What if I cannot cope?" To tackle unhelpful thinking it is important that all questions are changed into statements. So in this case, "What if I cannot cope?" should be changed to "I cannot cope!" – then it can be addressed more directly.

Everybody has thinking errors, whether depressed, anxious, suffering from low moods, or just when an upsetting circumstance happens. However, the depressed person is likely to have them more often. Almost constantly! They chip away at their self-esteem and sense of self until it makes the depressed person wish they could stay in bed all day.

It is beneficial to be able to recognise what type of thinking error the depressive is having. If the person undertaking this exercise cannot name the thinking error they are having, then simply acknowledge that these thoughts are unhelpful thoughts and help the client to understand that they are not one hundred percent true all of the time.

Here are the most common thinking errors I have seen with my clients:

Black and white thinking

This is also known as 'all or nothing' thinking. By this I mean that thoughts are either right or wrong, good or bad. There is no middle ground. They are one extreme or the other. For the depressed person a common thought is "I am a failure!" or "I cannot cope!"

Over-generalising

This generally means that a thought (based on one single piece of evidence) leads to the conclusion that everything will be in a certain way. A good example of this kind of thought in a depressive is "If I do not do x then my life will always be this way!" or more specifically "If I do not make a go of this relationship, then I will always be lonely!"

Catastrophising

This is very common in anxious individuals. This is where people overestimate the chances of something bad happening. Here the individual thinks something awful is imminent. Often these thoughts start with the words "What if". For example, "What if my tyre bursts, I come spinning off the road, hit a tree and die?"

Personalising

This is where the person takes responsibility for something that is *not* their fault or when they think something is to do with them - when it is not. A good way to spot people who personalise things is by spotting individuals who tend to apologise all the time.

Fortune telling

Rather self-explanatory - this is where we think we can tell what is going to happen. Somehow the depressive thinks that they have some form of psychic ability and feel as though they can predict the future when really they cannot. A good example for a depressive is: "If I go there then I *will* have a panic attack."

Should statements

This is when people tell themselves that they "should do this" or they "should do that". In doing so they put exceedingly large amounts of pressure on themselves which is not good for mental health. A good example for the depressive is "I should not get angry!" If they start to get angry, well, anxiety can kick in in a big way.

As I have said before, we can all have thinking errors. However the depressed person has them rather frequently. Once we have identified them as errors, we can now challenge them to help give the person more balance.

The ABC Model and Bringing Balance to Your Thoughts

This exercise is an adaptation of work undertaken by Tanner and Bail (1989). No matter how hard we try, we cannot control every situation around us. Sometimes, things simply just happen and we have no say in it. Should we feel affected by this situation, it is because it evoked some kind of thought and associated feeling. This was seen in the ABC model discussed in the "working with violent offenders" chapter 5.

So, for the depressive, we can use the same model to help counter situations that cause negative thoughts and feelings. In order to explain how to do this, I will use a working example of one of my old cases Billie, a 47 year old, black female.

Let us assume that client Billie is walking home from work. Billie's friend (who she works with) walks past and does not say hello and Billie feels ignored. She begins to think "she does not like me" and this evokes negative feelings of anger and sadness. The consequence of this is that Billie is late going to work the next day after spending the evening in floods of tears (she spent the whole night in the depressive cycle).

Here is how to record it in the ABC model:

A (Situation)	B (Thoughts)	Feelings	C (Consequence)
"My friend ignored me in the street"	"She does not like me"	Sadness (90)	Late for work the next day
		Angry (80)	Tears

Note: we should score feelings with regards to intensity (out of 100). By doing this we can see how effective the following skill you are going to use is.

After we have recorded the incident as in the table above, the depressive should start with the thought that has had the most impact on them. So in Billie's case this was "She does not like me." I shall now introduce a methodology to help bring balance and perspective to Billie's thinking.

Bringing Balance

In order to bring balance to Billie's thinking we need to dispute all the thinking errors she has. But I recommend that you start with the strongest. Disputing *all* the thinking errors is important as any error, on its own, can cause her upset and influence behaviour.

In order to dispute thinking errors we need to learn how to challenge thoughts. The practitioner should ask the client (Billie) the following in relation to the thinking error:

1. Is your thought a thinking error?
2. Is this thought a fact or an opinion? Here you may need to point out that a fact is something that is one hundred percent true and an opinion is not.
3. What are the other ways you could potentially look at the situation? Here you will need to point out that the alternative does not have to be true, just generate different ways of thinking about what happened.
4. If your thoughts are true, what action can be taken to help resolve the matter?

In order to answer these questions, we write them down in another column next to the ABC. Like this:

C (Consequences)	Challenging questions answers
Late for work the next day.	Q1.
	Q2.
Tears	Q3.
	Q4.

Here is how Billie answered the questions in this example:

1. Is your thought a thinking error? Yes – it is black and white thinking.
2. Is this thought a fact or an opinion? It's an opinion. I cannot prove one hundred percent that she did see me.
3. What are the other ways to look at the situation that caused these feelings and thoughts? Maybe she did not see me. Maybe she was in a rush. Maybe she thought I was ignoring her!

   Remember: the tip here is to put the word 'maybe' onto the front of the viewpoint.

4. If your thoughts are true, what action can bet taken to help resolve the matter? Talk to her, ask a friend if she is talking to me, write her an email.

After Billie has answered these questions, she needs to be asked how she now feels. Expressed feelings should have scored a lot less (sadness 20 and anger 10, for example), and new feelings such as relief (40) and happiness (10) should be present. These should be recorded in a new column.

C (Consequences)	Challenging questions	New feelings
Late for work the next day	1) Yes – it is black and white thinking 2) It's an opinion. I cannot prove 100 % that she did see me. 3) Maybe she did not see me. Maybe she was in a rush. Maybe she thought I was ignoring her! 4) Talk to her, ask a friend if she is talking to me, write her an email.	Sadness (20) Angry (10) Relief (40) Happiness (10)

The reason this approach works is because it shifts the individual's way of thinking away from a focus on the negative to a more balanced viewpoint. Now it may be the case that Billie's friend *is* actually ignoring her, but at least by using this method, Billie feels some form of relief away from her negative feelings. Additionally, she has also thought of a few ways to resolve the potential issues of her friend ignoring her.

And there we have it, the balancing questions! This approach may not work for all clients, especially those who are dismissive of CBT tools. But at least give it a go. It can be very powerful for those individuals that do use it.

This exercise can be quite long. However it is important that it is done to the best of your ability. This methodology is teaching a new way of thinking to the client, so try to encourage them to practice it when dealing with negative thoughts. Remember, teaching the offender these tools is part of your role.

Finally, I would like you to consider this one last point, and in my mind this is true for all of us, especially those who are depressed or who suffer from low moods. True relief from depression and low mood, as well as becoming happy within yourself, is not something that other people can make happen for you, nor is it something you can obtain from an external source. True happiness and pulling through depression comes as a result and product of living well. By this I mean, having a good quality of life and bringing balance to negativity. This can be achieved by changing the way we think and behave.

Summary

Understanding and learning to deal with emotional problems is a skill that can be taught and learnt. However, it is difficult and requires dedication by those attempting it. The client or person undertaking the intervention needs to be motivated to see the long term gains. Remember - "motivation follows action" - so clients need to start somewhere and if they do they will see benefits. If the above method helps someone deal with one negative thought then, in my opinion, the whole exercise was worth it.

When addressing offenders (and others) with depression or anxiety – a few areas stand out. Firstly, routine is good. This helps keep people in balance with their responsibilities and helps give them purpose. Secondly, exercise is brilliant for helping fight anxiety and depression. Thirdly, it is crucial to 'look after oneself'. If you cannot look after yourself then how can you look after anyone else? And lastly, always be kind to yourself if feeling low; try to find balance in thinking.

Some of this chapter might have come across as a self-help manual but it is hoped that practitioners will find it useful both for working with clients, and potentially for themselves. I have seen a high proportion of offenders and colleagues become unwell with depression, stress and anxiety, and it is important that we practice what we preach.

In the next chapter, we shall look at how to safeguard yourself as a practitioner.

8
Tips

Up until this point, my emphasis has been predominately on exploring factors linked to offending behaviour and exercises designed to help elicit change in offenders. In the last chapter however, you may have noticed a slight shift in attention. This shift was a movement away from the offender and a push towards the wellbeing of the practitioner as well.

In this chapter I will be taking this one step further. Here, I will be exploring some of what I feel are the best methods to safeguard yourself as a practitioner who works with individuals involved in antisocial behaviour. To do this, I'll offer core tips to help the practitioner survive in roles across a spectrum of professions that work directly with assisting offenders to change. For example, I will forewarn you of some of the challenges you may face, and address how you can best look after yourself when dealing with these challenges.

This chapter is important, and this is why! To any individual who works with offenders on a regular basis you need to be able to look after yourself. Otherwise, *how can you look after others*?

So here are some of my final pieces of advice.

Be an Expert and Manage Feelings

Learning to breathe in a conscious manner is one effective way to relieve some of the stress of life (I shall show you an exercise to do this later). However until then, it is important that we learn how to manage feelings – both for the practitioner and the offender.

Feelings are normal, and when a negative event happens this will sometimes result naturally in negative feelings. I have stressed this point throughout this book. But as a professional, do not think you this does not apply to you. Also, do not be ashamed to feel and express these feelings. In fact, I would argue that we cannot properly overcome issues such as bereavement, work stresses, and difficult life events without truly going through all the emotions that these events trigger. At the risk of sounding rather Freudian - too many people bottle up their emotions and feelings. In my experience, when people do this, feelings simply stay in their subconscious and the individual will usually express unexpressed emotion in negative ways such as through aggression. And yes, I said subconscious. I am sure it is there!

When coping with negative feelings, you do not have to go through them alone. Too many people think it is weak to express yourself, but it is not! Do not be ashamed to express how you feel to a colleague you trust and respect, or a supervising manager.

Experiencing feelings and overcoming them is especially pertinent to practitioners who work one-to-one with offenders. Often, an offender can project many negative feelings onto the practitioner; they 'offload' their own thoughts and emotions. On occasion, for example, after believing you did a great session with an offender the week before – they fire out something to the effect of: "You are just not helping me - this is a waste of time, I hate coming here!" The wind can be blown straight out of you as the practitioner and yet, in contrast, the offender feels fine and sometimes even happy. Negative feedback can have a very powerful effect on us, and if we do not know how to effectively deal with the feelings such comments can evoke then we may get trapped into the depressive cycle (discussed in chapter seven) or we could simply lose a little self-esteem and confidence in our abilities.

But fear not, and try to remember this: *an offender may very well try to project their feelings onto you; this should actually be expected when working with them.* Furthermore, in the world of psychology (psychotherapy anyway) this projection of emotions and feelings is seen as a critical part of treatment. It is formally known as *transference.* The practitioner should also be aware that transference can even occur the other way around and this is known as *counter transference.* The officer can project feelings and emotions they have about someone else (from their past) onto the offender. So it is important to discuss your feelings regularly with your manager.

So how do we know when transference happens - what are the signs? Well, in my own practice with offenders, transference often shows itself in the form of what can seem as extreme dependency. A good example of this is when the client tends to turn up at the office every day, without an appointment, just to tell you what they are doing even when it is not linked to what you have asked them to do. In this situation, it comes across to the onlooker as though the offender has placed you on a pedestal. In other cases, transference can manifest itself in completely the opposite way. Here the offender shows total mistrust in you, the 'system' and other professionals. They can even express anger towards you for what seems like no particular reason. In young offenders, I find this particularly common. They will attend their appointments and suddenly switch from being placid to angry and uninterested in a second.

Other key signs to look out for are:

- An erotic attraction towards a practitioner or therapist
- Rage
- Hatred

In all these situations, ensure that you plan for them by talking to your manager or an experienced practitioner. They may come up with great suggestions to manage these situations as well as providing safety advice that you have not thought of before.

The process of transference in psychotherapy, and with one-to-one offender supervision (in my view), is seen as important step which needs to happen and which needs to be addressed in some form for successful treatment. So again, talk to someone you trust when you recognise the signs above if you are transferring *your* feelings.

In the meantime, I would like to offer you a strategy for coping with emotions taken from my personal experience of learning to cope with stress and dealing with negative feelings. It is actually quite simple and involves you identifying coping strategies for yourself. See, you knew the answers all along!

Before we start, however, I would like you to remember that when you feel upset by something, no matter how long the emotion is held, it is only temporary. The brain has a natural ability to help you overcome matters over the long-term to the point where any period of negative emotion can just feel like a vivid memory and a learning experience. Do not be scared to feel sad. It is normal for a short period of time.

Coping Strategy

Step 1. With a friend, manager, or colleague you trust, both of you list all the types of positive and negative feelings you can think of. For example, happy, sad, etc.

Step 2. Now consider how you deal with each emotion in a positive and constructive way - a way in which you can manage each emotion so it does not become overwhelming. For example, using exercise to deal with stress, and meeting up with friends when happy.

Step 3. Compare the ways you deal with these emotions and think about other constructive ways to cope with them. Have you learnt anything new from each other?

Chapter 8

Once you have been able to identify the ways in which you can handle positive and negative emotions, it is important that we learn how to *maintain* our emotional wellbeing. One way to do this is by creating our own emotional maintenance plan. In order to do so, you need to give an example from each category listed below as to how you could maintain emotional wellbeing over the long term. So with this in mind here is a structure you can use:

Emotional Maintenance Plan questions

1. *Which people or person would you turn to, to help you maintain good emotional wellbeing?*

      Names:

      Why them:

2. *What place or places could you go to, to help you maintain good emotional wellbeing?*

      Places:

      Why here:

3. *What activities could you do to help maintain good emotional wellbeing?*

      Example:

      Why this:

4. *Which organisations could you go to, to help maintain good emotional wellbeing?*

      Names:

      Why them:

5. *What can you do to chill out and relax?*

      Example:

      Why this:

Be Prepared

In roles that address offending behaviour, the saying: [if you] *"fail to prepare then prepare to fail"* is never truer. Being prepared cannot be stressed enough. This applies to one-to-one sessions, visits, meetings, or any situation in the working environment.

Tip: On the note of visits, especially home visits, always and I mean *always* go with a colleague. You could be putting yourself at risk going alone.

Okay, so why have I said this? And why is it so important? Well, in order to answer the first question, I would like us to reflect on a case of mine.

I was working with Kat, a white female offender, who was aged around 40 years old. Her offence was common assault as well as several minor thefts. She was serving a one year community based sentence of one-to-one supervision with me. Much of her offending was based around alcohol abuse. She had previously been diagnosed as an alcoholic and had frequented residential rehabilitation.

Initially, Kat was very chaotic in her behaviours; however the residential setting saw her begin to abstain from alcohol. Everything was going well. She secured herself a job and she gained control of her finances which had once been a major issue for her. On top of this, she had also not touched alcohol (significantly linked to her offending) for several months.

One morning, my phone rang. It was reception. Reception told me that Kat had come in and wanted to see me. They also stated that she was acting a bit strange. I did not think anything of it. Initially I thought that Kat had just come in to let me know how she was getting on. She would often do this.

I went downstairs to the reception, did not take any security alarms, and failed to look at the records which I would usually do. I opened the door to let her into the interview room. Immediately I was engulfed by an overpowering smell of alcohol. In front of me stood Kat, swaying from side to side and in her hand was a bag full of bottles of vodka. I was shocked, and said the first thing that came to my mind. "Kat, what has happened?" The next thing I knew? A fist came flying towards my face with Kat shouting "I fucking give up!"

The punch would have hit me if it had not been for the rather John Wayne like style punch. Her arm went all the way back in slow motion and her fist headed towards me at a snail's pace.

> I took hold of Kat and walked her out of the building with a colleague who just happened to be in the same area. We then managed to calm her down and get her home before we started to tackle her relapse.

Reflecting on how this situation was managed, some important learning points become apparent about why it is important to prepare. Critically, by being prepared, the situation could have been avoided altogether.

Firstly, I could have asked the receptionist "How is she acting strange?" Then I may have been able to have foreseen her likely emotional state. Also, I should have looked at her records before going in to see her. By doing this, I would have been able to pick up on the fact that she had just lost her job and a colleague of mine had recorded this the previous day. If I had noticed this, then I would have been able to recognise that this situation (given her history) may have caused her frustration, and stress resulting in a possible lapse. At previous times, similar situations had generated immediate lapses.

Finally, I should have taken my panic alarm into the meeting but my arrogance did not permit me at the time. But I guess it was not simply arrogance at the time that stopped me. In my experience, as practitioners become more experienced, we can become more blasé about risk. We can spend too much time trying to separate the behaviour (offending) from the person and as such we potentially forget what risk clients pose. This becomes an even greater problem when we overlook the fact that some clients will have violence or sex offences on their record.

Taking panic alarms is standard protocol in many services across the UK. Should a colleague not have been close by then I possibly would not have been able to obtain support. So, be prepared. *Be as prepared as you can for every situation.*

How can you do this? Well, I could probably write a whole book on identifying situations and how to prepare for them. And I guess you cannot realistically prepare for everything, however, in short, I would recommend that you at the very least follow these points:

- Familiarise yourself with your local office's or organisation's protocols and policies - and follow them.
- Do your research on your offenders. What are their triggers? What are their factors related to offending?
- Prepare your sessions for every offender where you can. This gives the client clear direction and your session a purpose.

Tip: Try to incorporate all the different learning styles into one session. Also, remember to take some time to reflect on previous sessions to see what you can take forwards.

Before we move on, on the point of familiarising yourself with local policies, reading them may seem laborious but they are there for a good reason. Usually they have been written because someone before you has been in a difficult situation and it may well be similar to a position you find yourself in.

Be Flexible and Professional in Your Thinking

Never assume you know everything. Be flexible in your thinking. As we live we learn! Actually, let me rephrase that. "As we live we can learn *if* we allow ourselves to."

As practitioners, with the right training, we can make very accurate predictions on the likelihood of an offender re-offending and the risk they pose. However no assessment is definitive. We make assessments through theoretical profiling, assessment tools (static and dynamic), and professional judgement. Experience and years in these professions will give practitioners a confidence in making these assessments. However, as I have stated before in this book, and as my mentor once told me: "Once you think you know everything then you have lost touch with your role."

Many times throughout my career, I have seen the damage that rigid thinking (the polar opposite to flexible thinking) can have on not only offenders but professionals as well. By getting feedback and advice from other professionals this will always keep us grounded. So how does this rigid thinking develop in professionals?

In my experience, one of the reasons this can occur is because, over time, a practitioner will have to make many important decisions that have significant effects on not only the offender but also the community. Here the professional may become used to making many of the same formulated defensible decisions and so, when a similar situation arises, rather than thinking 'outside the box' and treating each situation as individual and unique they jump to the same conclusion as they did before. In fact, what should happen is that the professional should go through the process of using all the relevant tools first.

There is, however, another reason why professionals can become rigid in their thinking. We can simply become desensitised to what he hear. We sometimes forget what a massive impact some of the decisions we have to make can have on our offenders and the community. In many ways this is probably a defence mechanism we adopt to cope with the harsh realities of addressing offending behaviour.

In my view, decisions should always be based on a combination of assessment tools working together with previous experience. This is professional judgement at its best and professional decision making. Additionally, this also means that when a decision is made, a justifiable reason can be given to explain why we have taken a specific course of action. Then should questions be directed towards the practitioner by managers or auditors (internal and external) we can be confident with our reasoning. But remember, when we make a decision, we should record our thinking and the reasons behind any decisions in whatever computer system your organisation uses to record actions for your cases. A quote some of my colleagues have used in the past is: "If it is not written down then it did not happen!"

However, remember that whilst assessment tools are based on relevant research findings they are not 'fact'. They are statistical probabilities based on current and historical findings in research. Additionally, these assessment tools will change over time. So try to keep up with the times and maybe consider doing additional research in your spare time.

Going back to the point of rigid thinking - I have seen how constant defensible decision making can (on occasion) make the practitioner come across as overly defensive and sometimes overly vocal with their opinions especially when discussing a case with someone else. You will see that this happens a lot. Trust me!

Looking at this from the flip side, some practitioners express views to others, when not directly involved in a case, in the belief that they are helping. Then they dig their heels in and insist their point is correct, even when counter arguments carry more weight, in order to avoid 'looking bad'.

What seems to be missed here is that this job is not about winning arguments or remaining dogmatic – it is about eliciting positive change. Here is the case of Jade to illustrate, in part, the problems of rigid thinking and differences in opinion:

Jade was a young person known to the organisation I had been employed by for some time.

Jade had been working with a particular worker for over a year. He was on bail for a serious offence of Grievous Bodily Harm. He denied his offence throughout his bail period up until his trial when he eventually pleaded guilty. This worker was shocked that he did this. In fact they were almost convinced that he did not do the crime - having worked with him for over a year.

I was allocated to the case to prepare a Pre-Sentence Report to assist the courts in sentencing Jade. In interview, Jade made full admissions to me about what he had done. As such I wrote about this and made an assessment based on my findings. In my report, I identified him as being high risk to the public of committing a serious violent offence.

All Pre-Sentence Reports are 'gatekept'. This means that a senior practitioner or colleague will read the report to double check everything. On this occasion, Jade's worker was one of those individuals. Jade's worker battled with me saying that Jade was a "nice kid" and would "become worse if he went to

---

prison."

I asked why my colleague felt this way. The worker stated that he "…just knew him, and that this was a one off," and once again that Jade was not a high risk of harm. Again I asked why. My colleague said that he had assessed him as a medium risk of harm and that Jade should be managed in the community. I then presented the worker with some new information. Jade had been charged with an alleged rape and an alleged further serious assault for which he was awaiting a trial date. Additionally, in interview Jade had spoken to me about many fights he had been in involving gang related behaviour and the use of weapons. Still however, my co- worker was convinced that he was right and approached senior management to get me to change my assessment.

In conclusion, Jade received a lengthy custodial sentence. He was subsequently convicted of the further offences which added time to his sentence.

When looking back the above episode, I did in fact question and reflect on my assessment (which I was taught to do). But in this case I 'stuck to my guns' as I had evidence to back up my views as well as much more disclosure from the young person to base my decisions on. Later, it transpired that the court agreed with my risk assessments and proposals, so I can only go by this to recognise that my assessment was accurate and well received.

At a later point, my colleague revealed that he felt my assessment (which was so different to his) put his professionalism in question, and he did not like how this young person had lied to them for over a year.

Conclusively, it is my view, that by being overly defensive and rigid in our views, the decisions we make can have significant effects on ourselves, how others see us, our offenders' lives, and the way in which we protect the public.

Be Assertive and Confident

Previously in this book, I have explored the importance of being assertive. This is vitally important for our ability to communicate effectively with other professionals and offenders. It is also important in building our own self-esteem. By building our own self-esteem, a snowball effect is created. As our self-esteem grows, we will feel more confident. Then, as we feel more confident, the more assertive we become and so on.

So, through reflective learning, what can we learn if we are not assertive? Immediately, we can say that the long term effects of not being assertive will be a loss of self-esteem because we may not be able to express ourselves. A loss in self-esteem may also mean a loss in confidence, and when working with offenders this loss in confidence could lead others to question our ability to make important decisions - this even includes the offenders themselves. For example, in the example above of Jade, if I was not confident about my decision then it could have led the courts to feel that my assessment was flawed and as such, this could have resulted in a lesser sentence for Jade - putting the public at risk.

Let us move away from offenders for a second. Being confident and assertive in our own abilities is important when looking after ourselves. By being assertive, we create an insulator against stress. And in roles that work with offenders, being able to deal with stress is a huge factor.

So now you may ask - how do I become more assertive and confident? As professionals, it is important to be able to identify situations that we feel least and most comfortable in. So, my advice, is to list on a piece of paper what you think are your strengths and your weaknesses. Then ask your manager to do the same for you. Following this, compare the results. Straightaway, you may find that others have seen something in you that you did not see before - thus building your self-esteem a little. Additionally, others may corroborate what you do and this will re-affirm your own positive beliefs.

After this is done, it is important to do something about your weaker areas. Reflect on how you could improve as a practitioner. Think about what did not work and why. How could things be done differently? What has worked for others? And then maybe give this a go?

Tip: These kinds of discussions can also be had in what is known as *practice meetings*. This is where we have a formal discussion about a tricky case with our colleagues and managers to come up with new ways of working and managing the case.

The important thing when doing this exercise is not to pick holes in your practice but to look at *how* to improve it.

When working with offending behaviour do not let your confidence take a tumble when you feel that you do not have the answer or when someone reoffends. Remember, there is never, in this line of work, a definitive answer but best results can be achieved through trial and error. One size does not fit all.

To help you be more assertive, here are a few suggestions that can help improve your practice with your offenders and other professionals:

1. Be specific about what you want to say and express it in a clear and polite manner. When doing this it is important to make sure that what you are saying is as brief as possible to avoid 'losing people'. It is also important not to apologise

for expressing how you feel. Why should you be sorry for doing this? It is how you feel right?

2. It is perfectly okay to say 'No!' But be polite! Saying no is not rude or aggressive. It is our right. Saying no is not selfish or uncaring. Also, saying no does not mean that people will not like us. Others have a right to ask, you have the right to say no. In refusing other people's requests it is important to understand that you are not rejecting them as a person. There are many ways of saying no, however my favourite way when working with other professionals is to say no and *explain* (in brief) *why*. When working with offenders often reflective no(s) are good to use. An example of this is: "I understand that you wanted me to accept your reason for not attending, but I cannot as it is insufficient - as I explained when you started your order."

3. Use negative inquiries. This is a great skill for finding out if other people's criticism of your behaviour is actually constructive. Please use this or give it a go! Here is how it works. Your colleague has suggested that you are shy, so simply ask them: "In what ways do you think I am shy?" If you believe what they say is valid, then use this constructively. If they cannot respond, then it is likely that there is no substance to what they are saying.

Learn to Prioritise

It is Monday and a report you need to complete is due in on Thursday. You have two home visits this week, eight offenders to see, two multi-agency meetings on Tuesday afternoon, and now a case of yours has just turned up and said they are homeless. What do you do first?

Learning to prioritise is critical in roles that work with offenders. You will not survive in this line of work should you not become effective at scheduling and prioritising. So how do you schedule?

Well at the very basic end of things it is being able to keep an up-to-date diary of your movements. This includes a diary of who you are seeing, when you have any meetings, and lastly when you have any reports due. If you can, you should provide this in both a hard diary and on a shared data drive with your colleagues. However, I have found keeping a hardcopy diary and sending out emails of my schedule and movements is equally effective.

Tip: Keeping an up-to-date diary makes things less stressful for you and those who you work with when you may be sick or on leave. It helps to track your movements and others can rearrange any commitments you have such as appointments with offenders.

How do you prioritise? Very simply, I have always prioritised reports first and foremost along with high risk cases. Everything else is second. It is best to keep your philosophy as simple as you can so you do not get caught up in local office debates about what their priorities are. However, in saying this, it is also important to understand what your organisation's vision and priorities are. By knowing them, when you have addressed your reports and high risk cases, then you can focus on its issues.

Know the Basics of Cognitive Behavioural Therapy (CBT)

In the early phases of this book, I described some of the basic fundamentals of CBT. Given that CBT is the foundation of current effective practice in working with offending behaviour then I would suggest that every opportunity is taken to become as familiar with it as possible. This can include training courses offered by your organisation or even self-learning. Many books can be purchased from local bookstores under the self-help section.

When thinking about CBT, I like to remember that no matter what the exercise is, it is basically helping an individual control thoughts, feelings or behaviour. Remember that thoughts, feelings and behaviour are always linked. This is the whole idea of CBT in the first place.

A practitioner who works with offending behaviour may become confused with all the different work tools that may be available to them from various sources. Find which exercises work best for you and your offenders. Addressing offending behaviour is not a proven exact science and there is no prescriptive remedy that can 'cure it'. You need to learn to pick and choose exercises that can help your client.

Tip: Do not forget to ask for feedback on effectiveness from the client - it is a two way street.

Of course there are numerous forms of programmes that are available to practitioners and clients. Many clients may even be sentenced to them. However, structured interventions are there to help offenders build tools for their 'mental tool box'. You need to help them keep learning and practicing. And as stated above, this may mean that you should find new exercises to do with them, or review old ones.

Breathe and Change

Learning to cope with what life throws at you is an important part of learning how to work with offenders. After all, part of pro social modelling is actively showing what behaviours you want others to mimic.

It is natural to feel low and sad from time to time, and of course you cannot ever be fully prepared for all occurrences. For example, some people may have to cope with a number of major events happening at the same time; some people may experience events such as divorce or ending a relationship, bereavement, or loss of employment all in the space of a few months. The good news, however, is that you can learn skills to help support yourself through difficult times. Once mastered, you can show these to other people and even your clients.

On a very basic level, it is important to recognise that life changes all the time, and as life changes these events can cause us stress because (in our minds) it is sometimes 'safer' for us to stay where we are.

Generally, you could say that the more change we face - the greater the likelihood of stress if we do not embrace it. But stress is normal. It is only when you believe it affects you physically or emotionally that it should be considered a problem. When considering the link between change and stress, we need to recognise that we cannot always stop change - even if we want too. What we can do, however, is learn to cope with it. This is a skill.

Learning to cope with change can be as simple as breathing. In fact, learning to breathe is what I would like to talk about. This is because learning to breathe properly, in a controlled way, will help you overcome and deal with some of the initial negative symptoms of stress.

Here is an exercise I would like you to try when you begin to feel the stress of change.

Learning to Breathe

Step 1. Understand that when you experience stress, especially unwanted stress, your breathing naturally changes. This is a normal body function. You are no different to anyone else.

Step 2. Recognise that when you are stressed, you can become easily distracted, lose concentration and even begin to panic.

Step 3. When this happens, recognise the symptoms. Find a quiet space or quiet area and sit or lie down. If you really try, you can do this anywhere. Yes, even at work.

Step 4. Close your eyes and begin to concentrate on your breathing.

Step 5. Focus on your breathing.

Step 6. Take deep breaths. I like to count four seconds of inhalation through my mouth, and five out through my nose. If you do it the other way around it does not really matter, e.g. through your nose first. Just concentrate and take deep breaths. Really focus on the breathing.

Step 7. Keep breathing this way, and begin to notice how calm you are becoming. Notice how your body is beginning to change and become calm and in tune with itself again. Allow this to happen, because it will. Only finish the exercise when you feel you have become calm again. Try it, it really can work.

Note: When doing this exercise you will notice that your mind will wander from time to time. I will probably start by thinking "Why am I doing this?" or "I look stupid!" Or maybe even "Have I paid my bills yet?" This is normal. Just gently and calmly re-focus on your breathing as soon as you realise what you are doing. The more you practice this, the less you will think about all the other aspects of life.

You may ask yourself: "I might be able to do this, but how would this work with my offenders?" Well the truth, more often than not, is that when you try to teach this skill to a group of offenders they can be dismissive of it. This is their individual choice. Your role is to simply teach them the tools that work and encourage them to use them as best you can. So, how better to promote it than by doing it yourself?

Tip: Sometimes an offender will laugh at the idea of this exercise. Roll with this resistance and go with the laughter and ask them to keep practicing it - they may never admit it but some offenders will then go away and use it.

Do Not Be Scared to Change

If I can promise you anything, then this is it. Change will happen! This applies to everything we do. It is applicable to the organisation you work in, our lives, and our offenders. Understanding this is important - if we do not adapt to change then we will not move forward. For example, let's assume that your role has now changed from a group work facilitator to a one-to-one case manager because of financial costs to the organisation. In this situation, you can respond in several ways. You can begrudge the move, or you can accept it. What would you do?

Before you answer this, I would like you to consider your own personal reasons for why you are in this occupation (or would consider a role in this occupation). Generally is because you wanted to help people right? Now answer this, with the ꓵned role change - are you not helping people in a new way? Why not give ꓵne case manager role a go? You could learn something new or maybe even

So do not be scared of change, try to enjoy it. Consider the amount of energy you are wasting trying to resist it if you do not want change to happen. You could be focusing it elsewhere in a more productive way. We cannot predict what is around the corner much of the time but we can anticipate and prepare for any obstacles that we think we may face.

With the role change example, it is highly unlikely that it would have just suddenly happened. As a practitioner, you would have been notified in advance. Should you not wish to follow this path, and adapt to this change, then why would you not look for another role that meets your personal needs? After all it is important to keep searching for what *you want* otherwise you may become upset and frustrated about your situation. Sometimes I like to think to myself - what would I do if I was not afraid of what lies ahead? Then I do it!

Take Regular Breaks

Taking breaks may seem like common sense but you would be surprised by how many practitioners I have seen not take them. Sometimes practitioners can be so passionate and dedicated to their roles that they often miss their lunch breaks or work into the late hours of the evening. However, taking breaks does not mean you are not passionate about your job. Taking breaks makes you more effective.

It is everybody's personal decision how to work within the framework of their contractual obligations. However, I believe it is important to take breaks and get into a routine. One good friend told me that it is important to have a good work life balance and I wholeheartedly agree.

Often, when practitioners work in the way I have described above, they become overly stressed in the long term and this can translate itself into other parts of their lives such as fractures in their personal relationships. In some cases I have even seen overtiredness in practitioners causing depression.

So, my advice:

- Take regular breaks
- Eat well
- Listen to local policies about work hours and do not go above this where possible. They are there for a reason, believe it or not, to ensure that you have the appropriate work life balance.

You Are Unique

When working with offending behaviour, I feel that it is important to recognise what you, as an individual, bring to the job. Some of us may have qualities in building relationships with offenders while others appear to be experts in CBT. Use each other and learn off each other. Never forget what you are good at.

Tip: Although you are unique, never think that asking a colleague to step in or give you advice diminishes you as a practitioner. Sometimes it makes sense to have another opinion or someone else to work with an offender. Think of it as 'trading experiences' and that one day you will be there for that practitioner to repay the favour.

Every practitioner is different. We have all experienced different elements of what life has to throw at us. In many cases, we have pulled through and therefore we should seek to use these experiences alongside professional knowledge to help empathise with our clients.

Learning to empathise through our experiences of life is a critical skill when working with offenders. However, it is important to never fall into the trap of becoming what I call 'overly empathetic' – a state which could cloud objective judgement. For example, you may, as an individual, have experienced the hardships of financial turmoil. You may have even experienced and overcome not being able to afford to eat. Should you then work with an individual who is currently in this situation - you may be tempted to give them money for food. This does not solve the problem. In my experience, it is more beneficial to help equip that individual with the skills needed to overcome any given situation. For example, helping them find employment, or advice on money management, alongside support through food vouchers. By doing this, you are empowering them to change and not giving them a quick but temporary fix.

Build a Support Network

In roles where you may be working with individuals with complex and difficult backgrounds – a support network is crucial. Offenders may have experienced significant abuse and harm, they can struggle to express themselves, and after working with them for a long time, they may suddenly begin to 'open the flood gates' and you become overwhelmed by what you hear. How do you then handle this personally?

Due to confidentiality, you cannot really talk to anyone outside of work. Additionally, if you did talk to people about what you do on a day-to-day basis, many people will not understand. Or even worse, they will give you an opinion which totally confuses you. For example when trying to maintain balance it can become difficult when someone offers an opinion such as: "All sex offenders should be shot!"

To help you cope with this, I am of the view that all practitioners should build a positive support network, and then learn to express their feelings within it. Make sure, though, that the people you decide to bring into your support network are positive and constructive individuals.

One good way to create an effective support network is by developing good friendships with work colleagues who experience what you do. In turn, use your family, close friends and perhaps outside organisations that are there to help you (such as the Samaritans). Anyone can be in this network as long as they are positive.

So next time a colleague invites you for a coffee - why not make the effort?

Have Regular Supervision

In the last chapter, I spoke about the importance of supervision for practitioners. Here, I would like to reiterate this point.

Having regular supervision with your manager is a great way to ensure that you can obtain feedback and constructive advice on how to work with specific cases that concern you. Through supervision, managers should look to help practitioners reflect on their own practices, discuss issues with cases, and look to see how the practitioner is coping. In my opinion, supervision sessions should always be empowering and positive for the practitioner.

The problem here is that I have seen some practitioners fail to attend supervision appointments because they are "too busy". This may be true, but make time for it, it is important. Maybe if you did make the time, then perhaps this would make your job easier in the future.

As a practitioner - take some responsibility for making sure you have regular supervision. Some managers may forget, but this does not make them bad managers. Think about it. Who would you consider worse in this situation: the manager who genuinely forgot, or the practitioner who knew they had supervision due (and could have had it if they simply reminded the manager).

Tip: Make the effort to rebook your supervision with your manager regardless of the reason for it not happening as originally intended.

Chapter 8

Summary

Let us now go back to the introduction of this book and revisit the two critical questions. These being:

- How do we address offending behaviour?
- Why is offending behaviour so difficult to stop?

Unfortunately, there are no simple answers to these questions. In truth, these questions have only been partially answered in this book. The complexities of human behaviour far outweigh the evidence based research which has been put in place to address them. Ultimately, we can only do what we can with the knowledge that is available at the time.

Every individual is different. Their issues are unique and come in different combinations. Professionals need to learn to identify what these issues are and in what combination they interact. A bit like cooking. Put the wrong amount of something into your recipe and the outcome will not be what you want.

However, do not take on the idea that practitioners have to, and are responsible for, always getting it right or are responsible for an offender's decisions. At the end of the day, professionals can only ever give advice and support for an offender to overcome their problems. Professionals do not have some miracle cure. When all the chips are down, ultimately, it is up to the client or offender to pull through their difficulties. It is not the professional's responsibility to do the changing for people. In fact, they cannot. Professionals give the tools needed for change and the client should go out and try these new tools. Should a professional feel that it is their responsibility to actually change people, then this is a sure-fire way to set themselves and even offenders up to fail.

When considering the tools needed to evoke change, CBT alongside particular practitioner experiences is very effective in addressing some of the individual factors linked to offending behaviour. Behaviour is often an outcome of many factors. For example, failing to deal with stress may appear to be one reason an individual has offended, but other contributing reasons might include employment, dealing with relationships, and anger management. These dynamic factors may also change over time, and the practitioner needs to look to their relationship with their offenders to ensure that information is accurately conveyed, recorded and updated to make sure everything gets addressed appropriately. This will then help reduce an individual's likelihood of re-offending.

Initially in this book, I controversially spoke about the idea that offending behaviour can never really be fully grasped by professionals who have not experienced some connection with it. However, I do not take this viewpoint literally. I would argue that you do not fully need to understand the 'in's and outs' to effectively address offending. You just need to know about the possible connections and how to help people overcome their difficulties.

I hope that you have found this book insightful and interesting. Its intention is to give the novice practitioner or pending practitioner an overview and another perspective on what I have seen as being effective practice when working with offenders.

Lastly, good luck, and I would love to hear from any readers on how they have found this book. You can leave feedback in one of the forums on my website at: *www.reoffending.org.uk* or you can email me directly at: *intervention.consultant@ymail.com*

Should you want any further consultancy on how to address *any type* of offending behaviour then feel free to email me your questions at the email address above.

Bibliography

Bandura, A., Underwood, B. & Fromson, M.E. (1975) Disinhibition of aggression through diffusion of responsibility and dehumanization of victims. *Journal of Research in Personality*, 9, 253-269.

Burnett, R. & McNeil, F. (2005) The place of the officer-offender relationship. *The Journal of Community and Criminal Justice*, Vol 52 (3)1, Sage Publications.

Burns, D. (1990) *The Feeling Good Handbook: Using the new mood therapy in everyday life*. New York: Penguin/Harpers and Row.

Chapman, T. & Hough, M. (1998) *Evidence based practice: A guide to effective practice*. London: Home Office Publication Unit.

Dobash, R.P. & Dobash, R.E. (1998) *Rethinking violence against women*. London: SAGE Publications.

Dobash, R.P., Dobash, R. E., Cavanagh, K. & Lewis, R. (1996) *Re-educating programmes for violent men - an evaluation*. London: Home Office Research Findings Number 46. Home Office.

Dobash, R.P., Dobash, R. E., Wilson, M. & Daly, M. (1996) *The Myth of sexual symmetry in marital violence*. Social Problems, 39(1), 71-91.

Finkelhor, D. (1984) *Child sexual abuse: New Theory and Research*. New York: The Free Press.

Bibliography

Fleet, F. & Annison, J. (2003) In support of effectiveness: Facilitating participation and sustaining change, in W.H. Chui and M. Nellis (Eds.), *Moving Probation Forward: Evidence, Arguments and Practice.* Harlow, Essex: Pearson Education. pp.129-145.

Fleming, N. D. & Mills, C. (1992) Not another inventory, rather a catalyst for reflection. *To Improve the Academy*, 11(1) 1992, 137-144.

Gayford, J.J. (1995) Wife battering; a preliminary survey of 100 cases. *British Medical Journal*, 25(1), 94-97.

Giles-Sims, J. (1983) *Wife-beating: A system theory approach.* New York: Guilford.

Goldstein, D. & Rosenbaum, A. (1985) An evolution of the self-esteem of maritally violent men. *Family Relations*, 34, 425 - 428.

Gurbin, D. (1999) Actuarial and clinical assessment of risk in sex offenders. *Journal of Interpersonal Violence*, 14(3), 331-43.

Hanson, R.K. & Harris A. (1998) *Dynamic predictors of sexual recidivism.* Ottawa: Solicitors General of Canada.

Hart, B., Stuehling, J., Reese, M. & Stubbing, E. (1990) *Confronting domestic abuse: effective practice responses.* Pennsylvania: Pennsylvania Coalition Against Domestic Abuse.

Healey, K., Smith, C. & O'Sullivan, C. (1998) *Batterer intervention; Program approaches and criminal justice strategies.* National Institute of Justice.

Hopkinson, J. & Rex, S. (2003) Essential skills in working with offenders, in W. H. Chui & M. Nellis (2003) *Moving Probation Forward: Evidence Arguments and Practice.* Essex, UK: Pearson Longman.

Howell, M. & Pugliesi, K. (1998) Husbands who harm: Predicting spousal violence by men. *Journal of Family Violence*, 3(1), 15-27.

Kemshall, H. (1997) The dangerous are always with us: dangerousness and the role of the Probation Service. *VISTA*, 2(3), 136–53.

Kemshall, H. (2000) *Risk assessment and management of known sexual and violent offenders; a Review of current issues.* Police Research Series, HMSO.

Kropp, P. R., Hart, S. D. & Webster, C. W. (1995) *Manual for the Spousal Assault Risk Assessment Guide, 2nd edition.* Vancouver, BC: British Columbia Institute on Family Violence.

Mirrlees-Black, C. (1999) *Domestic violence: Findings from a new British crime survey self-completion questionnaire*, HO Research Study, 191.

Motiuk, L., Smiley, C & Blanchette, K. (1996) Intensive programming for violent offenders; a comparative investigation. *Forum on corrections research*, 8(3), 10-12.

NPS (2005) *National guide for the new Criminal Justice Act 2003 sentences for public protection.* London: NOMS.

O'Brien, J. (1971) Violence in divorce-prone families. *Journal of Marriage and the Family*, 33, 692-698.

Prochaska, J. & Di Clemente, C. (1984) *The transtheoretical approach: crossing traditional boundaries of therapy.* Homewood, IL: Dow Jones-Irwin

Rosenbaum, A. & O'Leary, D. (1981) Marital violence: characteristics of domestic abusive couples. *Journal of Consulting and Clinical Psychology*, 49, 663-7.

Serin, R.C. (1996) Violent recidivism in criminal psychopaths. *Law and Human Behaviour*, 20(2), 207-217.

Straus, M. A., Gelles, R.J. & Steinmetz, S.K. (1980) *Behind closed doors: Violence in the American Family*. New York: Doubleday/Anchor.

Tanner, S. & Bail, J. (1998) *Beating the Blues: A Self-help Approach to overcoming depression*. London: Sheldon Press.

Tardiff, K. (1984) Violence and Psychosis I - Risk of violence amongst psychotic men. *British Medical Journal*, 288, 1945 - 49.

Walby, S. & Myhill, A. (2000) Reducing Domestic Violence... What Works? *Policing and Reducing Crime Unit Briefing Note*. London: Home Office.

West, D. (1996) Sexual molesters. In N. Walker (Ed.) *Dangerous people*. London: Blackstone Press.

Winstone, J. (2006) *Research and Effective Practice*. Portsmouth: University of Portsmouth.

Winstone, J. & Hobbs, S. (2006) Motivational interviewing and the cycle of change. In J. Winston & S. Hobbs. (Eds.) Strategies for Tackling Offending Behaviour, 2(3), Portsmouth: University of Portsmouth. pp. 257-272.

Lightning Source UK Ltd.
Milton Keynes UK
UKOW022316211112

202576UK00005B/11/P